C000216307

Younis Ahmed played four Test matches for Pakistan, although there was a seventeen-year gap between the second and third – the result of a ban he received for touring South Africa during the apartheid era.
He played for Surrey for thirteen years, winning the County Championship in 1971. He also played for South Australia, Worcestershire and Glamorgan, scoring over 1,000 first-class runs in thirteen different seasons.
Younis now lives in Surrey with his wife, Puchi.

Lahore

To

London

YOUNIS AHMED

Chequered Flag
PUBLISHING

First published in the UK by Chequered Flag Publishing 2016
PO Box 4669, Sheffield, S6 9ET
www.chequeredflagpublishing.co.uk

A CIP record for this book is available from the British Library

Printed in the EU by Print Group Sp. z o.o.

ISBN 9780993215261

To Gloria, Puchi, my children and grandchildren.

Contents

INTERNATIONAL   WANDERERS

F. J. TWISELTON,
Upper Westcott,
Northview Road,
Budleigh Salterton,
Devon.
Home: Budleigh Salterton 2463
Office: Cheltenham 21401
Office: Tiverton 4921

JOINT MANAGERS

R. K. THOMAS,
"The Red Hart,"
Kington, Worcs.
Inkberrow 792-745
792-221

"Lower Kytes,"
Dormston, Worcs.
Inkberrow 792-442

Office: 7 Church Rd.,
Redditch, Worcs.
Tel. 63258

D. B. CLOSE (Captain)
ENGLAND, YORKSHIRE, SOMERSET

E. J. BARLOW
SOUTH AFRICA

A. S. BROWN
GLOUCESTERSHIRE

I. M. CHAPPELL
AUSTRALIA, SOUTH AUSTRALIA

G. S. CHAPPELL
AUSTRALIA, SOUTH AUSTRALIA, QUEENSLAND

A. W. GREIG
ENGLAND, SUSSEX

M. J. HARRIS
NOTTINGHAMSHIRE, MIDDLESEX

G. D. McKENZIE
AUSTRALIA, LEICESTERSHIRE, W. AUSTRALIA

R. G. POLLOCK
SOUTH AFRICA

B. A. RICHARDS
SOUTH AFRICA, HAMPSHIRE

G. R. J. ROOPE
ENGLAND, SURREY

P. J. SAINSBURY
HAMPSHIRE

J. N. SHEPHERD
WEST INDIES, KENT

J. SIMMONS
LANCASHIRE

R. W. TOLCHARD
LEICESTERSHIRE

G. M. TURNER
NEW ZEALAND, WORCESTERSHIRE

YOUNIS AHMED
PAKISTAN, SURREY

A signed squad list from my second tour to South Africa
– some of the sport's greats featured in it.

Preface

Peter Oborne's excellent history of Pakistan cricket is entitled *Wounded Tiger*. Imran Khan's ten-minute address to his team which was about to win the World Cup in 1992 encouraged them to 'fight like cornered tigers'. Tigers have a part in the national folklore in Pakistan. They are beautiful animals, but they do have a reputation for occasionally eating people.

I have enjoyed my life in cricket, both on and off the field, but there are times when my progress has been hampered; sometimes through my own actions, sometimes not. As I approach the end of my seventh decade, still involved with the game by doing a bit of coaching but with my professional playing career long over, I thought it was time to put my side of the story – to respond to my treatment by the Pakistan Cricket Board in handing me a life ban, Surrey's failure to grant me a benefit ahead of my peremptory dismissal, and Worcestershire's decision to not grant me a new contract. To those decisions I made no contribution. There are other instances too where I have been misjudged, through no fault of my own. It is time for the tiger to turn and bite back.

But my life has not been just reaction. Far from it. I believe most of it has been entirely proactive. In my teens I made a decision to come to England to try and make a career in cricket. A few years later, I made a more difficult decision, to join a tour to South Africa in the hope that I could make a contribution to promote multi-racial cricket in an era dominated by the evil of apartheid. I helped take international cricket to Dubai, have established coaching clinics to help future generations of cricketers and run two successful restaurants.

At one stage I thought about calling this book something like *Across the Colour Bar* and, while that might have been adequate for the South African section of the story, it is by no means the whole of it. It has been a wonderful journey from Lahore to London, though not by the most direct route. Adelaide, Johannesburg and Dubai would not normally be stopping off points on the way!

Any regrets? Perhaps I would have liked to play more international cricket – I believe that I was good enough to – but if I had done so, then I would have missed out in other areas. Although I did not expect my visit to South Africa in the apartheid era to be without consequences, I was not expecting a lifetime ban. And maybe I should have been more discerning in my choice of counties. Kent would have attracted me. But such decisions are easy with the benefit of hindsight. It has been said that life can be understood only looking backwards, but it has to be lived looking forwards, and decisions have to be made in the light of the circumstances prevailing at the time. So Surrey was the correct choice in 1965, even though by 1978 it would all turn a bit sour.

All that aside, cricket has enabled me to see different countries like India, England, South Africa, Rhodesia, Australia and the West Indies. Without it I would never have met Bollywood star Dilip Kumar, cricket legend Sir Donald Bradman and world statesman Nelson Mandela. There have been others too, both within the game and outside it. I thank them all for enriching my life – even those whom I am now biting back.

Younis Ahmed

Pakistan training camp in Karachi for present (back row)
and future (front row) internationals.
I am fifth from the right on front row.

1

Across the Frontier

Imran Khan bowls to Sunil Gavaskar – two legends of the game facing each other on the cricket field. The first ball of the first Test match ever to be played in Jaipur takes an inside edge, flies from the opener's new ultra-light pads, and is caught low down by my friend Javed Miandad at third slip. India are 0 for 1.

Forget The Ashes. For those born and reared on the sub-continent, India versus Pakistan is by far cricket's most significant international contest. And, at the age of almost forty, I am involved in it for the first time. I am playing for my homeland – or one of them – against the country of my birth.

I was born in Jullundur (now Jalandhar) in the Punjab on 20 October 1947. Just over two months earlier, on 15 August, most of the Punjab, including the largely Sikh community of Jullundur, had remained part of India after partition. I do not remember anything of Jullundur, as my

5

family moved from there when I was just three months old, across the recently drawn frontier to Lahore in the newly created Islamic Republic of Pakistan. Likewise, I have no memory of the move, but it must have been very difficult for my mother and father to move such a young family, at that time three sons and a daughter. At the time, Lahore's population was approaching one million. Almost seventy years later, it is more than ten times that.

Like Pakistan's other big cities, Lahore is a hotbed of cricket. There is a passion which can scarcely be imagined by those who have not experienced it. It was in its schools and streets that legends of the game like Lala Amarnath, Fazal Mahmood, Imtiaz Ahmed, Waqar Hasan, Waqar Younis, Wasim Akram and Saqlain Mushtaq first learned to play. Imran Khan, with both parents from Pathan land-owning families, lived in the upmarket Zaman Park district of Lahore – although, like me, he would not have played cricket in the street.

In one's early career, whether in sport, entertainment or business, mentors and advice from people with more experience of life are important. My early mentors were my father and eldest brother Saeed. Both instilled in me the value of hard work and taught me that success in any walk of life does not come by chance, but effort will be rewarded.

My father, Inyatullah Ahmed, worked for the Government's Diplomatic Service and was a keen cricketer, as were all of my five brothers. The eldest, Saeed – a full brother, not a half-brother as many sources incorrectly record – was the most successful on the cricket field. He was a top order batsman who represented Pakistan in forty-one Test matches, scoring 12,847 first-class runs at a career average of just over 40. He still holds the record for being the fastest Pakistan batsman to 1,000 Test runs. He passed that milestone in only his eleventh Test, the first eight of which were against the West Indies. In 1962, he was the recipient of the country's Pride of Performance Award, presented by Field Marshal Mohammad Ayub Khan, Pakistan's second President.

Apart from Saeed, I was the only brother to play first-class cricket, but the others were among the top ranks of club cricketers. Anwar was on the MCC groundstaff in the early 1970s at the same time as Ian Botham, later to become a legend of the game. I also have two sisters. We were a large happy middle-class family to which a loving mother devoted her full attention.

I never played street cricket. We were fortunate enough to occupy a large six-bedroom house with a lawn where my brothers and I would spend long hours playing the game, supervised by my father when he was not at work. The format was usually that we would each bat for ten overs; my father, who was also our coach and mentor, would umpire and keep the score. There would be a post-match analysis and sweets – methai, as they are known in Pakistan – for the winner.

My father emphasised that batting was like a battle and the batsman had to impose himself on the bowlers. The matting pitches of schools and club cricket offered turn and bounce and meant that virtually all teams had at least an off spinner, a leg spinner and a left-arm spinner. It was important to be able to defend against these, but also to attack, take them out of their comfort zone and cause them to change line, length and field. From a very early age, I learned to use my feet to attack spin bowling.

By the time I hit my teens, Saeed was already established on the first-class scene and no longer formed part of these backyard encounters. The age gap between Saeed and myself was ten years, so I never received any direct coaching from him, but we were immensely proud of him as he played for Punjab University and later for PIA – Pakistan International Airlines. The whole family, including the extended family of uncles, aunts and cousins, followed his progress in his first Test matches in the West Indies. There is a twelve-hour time difference between the subcontinent and the Caribbean and in those days there was no radio commentary, still less satellite television coverage, but nevertheless we had friends in the press who through the agency tapes kept us as up to date as possible. Throughout my early career he remained a tremendous inspiration, never more so than when the city of Lahore looked on in admiration as in 1959 he compiled 166 against the full might of Australia. It was a strong Australian line-up under the captaincy of Richie Benaud with an attack spearheaded by Alan Davidson and Ian Meckiff, Lindsay Kline and Benaud himself providing the spin support. Australia were well ahead on first innings and Saeed's six-hour innings almost salvaged a draw. It was the first Test match at what is now the Gaddafi Stadium and still remembered by many people in Lahore.

There may have been other things we did as a family, but I have no recollection of what they were. Talk round the dinner table and during leisure hours was of cricket and little else. My choice was between cricket and studying, and the latter came a poor second. Hockey is also a very popular sport in Pakistan, but as I am a natural left hander, it is not one that has commanded much of my attention.

My early cricket was with the Muslim Model High School and also the Crescent Club – then and now, in terms of size and success, one of the leading clubs in Lahore. School cricket is big in Pakistan, matches being often played over three or four days and declarations not permitted in the first innings. The system allows players time to mature and to develop the mentality of building long innings and giving bowlers the skills of persevering for long spells and earning their wickets. Our big rivals were Central Model, socially superior perhaps, but we liked to think we had the better cricketers. Certainly Muslim Model High has produced the greater number of Test cricketers over the years, including Arif Butt, Mohammad Ilyas and, in later years, Mudassar Nazar and Saleem and Aamir Malik.

Aitchison College, which has been called the Eton of Lahore, was for the sons of the British Raj and locals of higher social standing than the Ahmed family. It was private, better financed, and consequently had better facilities. It did not, however, produce many cricketers of quality. Imran Khan, one of its more successful alumni, has taken the view that the college failed to prepare its students for the intensity of international competition. It was too 'soft'. As well as Imran, Aitchison produced Wasim and Rameez Raja, but these were rare exceptions. Despite its outstanding playing and practice facilities, the main direction of its students was towards the upper echelons of government and business where there was money, rather than the cricket grounds of the country where there was not.

Batting for long periods in the back garden improved my concentration immensely. In one school match I scored 285 not out, spending almost two days at the crease. My father watched the entire match. He had given me an incentive – a new bat of my choice if I made a century. At 65 came the message that I was just 35 runs away from that new bat. There was no way I was going to get out. The century came and went, so did another, a third beckoned.

I had already developed the philosophy of Sir Donald Bradman – who I was to meet much later in my career – that a century is only the beginning. Why give it away? You're in and you're set. Take guard again and get another one. It was the kind of system, still used in schools cricket in Pakistan and India, which enabled Pranav Dhanawade to score an almost unbelievable 1,009 not out in January 2016, beside which the individual scores in the 200s, 300s and 400s which I experienced in my day pale into insignificance. It is a sharp contrast to what happens in England where some independent schools have played matches over two days in the past, but very few do now. In the state sector, only a minority of schools play the game anyway; those that do play perhaps over a day, but more often just a half day on a Twenty20 or similar limited overs basis.

My innings of 285 not out was not untypical and there is no way that English school cricket could produce a batsman such as Mohammad Iqbal (also known as Balla Natha) who scored 475 not out, an innings which continued into the third day, causing the match to be extended to a fourth. He later played first-class cricket and was on the fringes of the national side, playing for Pakistan Eaglets on their tour of England in 1959 under the captaincy of Saeed. I have always thought that he was tremendously unfortunate never to get the opportunity to play Test cricket, but he was a number three batsman and that slot was occupied by Saeed. On my recommendation he was invited to play a few matches for Surrey 2nd XI when he was in England in the early 1970s and Arthur McIntyre was coach. Then as now, 2nd XIs often found themselves in the position of having to find players at the last minute because of injuries and 1st XI calls and Mohammad was always happy to fill in at short notice. His first love was always cricket and he felt it a great privilege to represent Surrey 2nd XI.

Mohammad Iqbal and Mohammad Ilyas were both at my school, the latter as captain, where we were coached by Mr Naiz Rabbani. He was always tough and competitive and insisted that everyone, whatever their position in the batting order, had to have fifteen to twenty minutes in the net, facing the new ball. We then had to run round the ground with pads on and bat in hand, and he would monitor our speed. If at any stage we were going more slowly, he would make us go round again.

From Muslim Model High, I went on to Government College in Lahore where sporting achievements were useful additions to academic ones for admission requirements. I am proud to be one of a number of international cricketers to have attended that educational institution. Saleem Pervez, a cricket statistician from Pakistan, has recently produced some statistics on the number of cricketers from the college who have gone on to become first-class cricketers. Others were Mahmood Hussain, Waqar Hasan, Khalid Hasan, Shuja-u-din, Khalid Aziz, Saeed Ahmed, Javed Burki, Zafar Altaf, Pervez Sajad, Shafqat Rana, Asif Masood, Salim Altaf, Majid Khan, Waqar Ahmed, Aftab Gul and, not least, Mohammad Ilyas. We shall meet him later on several occasions. Of non-cricketing alumni, perhaps the best known is Prime Minister Nawaz Sharif.

I played club cricket with the Crescent Club in Lahore, which has produced many famous cricketers, including Lala Amarnath, India's first post-independence Test captain. Agha Saadat Ali, who had played a number of first-class matches including one Test match, was captain and coach and helped my technique and my concentration. He was a friend of many Test cricketers and a great adviser to me in my early days. He came from a privileged background, but most of the players were lower down the social scale and, unlike Lahore Gymkhana which had money and turf pitches, we had little money and matting pitches.

The club had three nets on four evenings of the week, Tuesday to Friday. Attendance was huge and at times unmanageable, each net having twenty or two dozen players. It was an indication of the enthusiasm for the game, although it did mean that some high-quality players who were not good at putting themselves forward might have been overlooked. As a junior player, I was always towards the end of the batting list. I did not mind that. It gave me an opportunity to watch the senior players and learn from them, players such as Salim Altaf who would later open both bowling and batting for Pakistan and later still become a selector and Chief Executive of the Pakistan Cricket Board.

Club cricket was different from schools cricket. Most of the playing members were working people, so matches were confined to weekends with the occasional midweek match. Karachi is the largest city in Pakistan and was the capital until 1967. There has always been rivalry between Karachi and Lahore, but there was more cricket in Lahore at the time – and Lahoris will tell you it was better cricket. There were around forty clubs, split into two divisions, of which Crescent was one of the leading ones with Universal and Mamdot as their main rivals, Mamdot especially as it was a club for rich men who considered themselves socially superior. The Wazir Ali League (called after the Indian Test batsman who after partition migrated to Pakistan) was split into two divisions and matches were played at Minto Park, beginning at 3pm on Saturdays after work and continuing from 7am on Sundays, each innings lasting a maximum of two and a half hours. The number of overs could vary but no one seemed to mind. Midweek matches were played over 45 overs per innings and later over 36 eight-ball overs. Finals were usually played over two days or to a finish. Until 1953/54 there had been no first-class structure and this was the highest standard at which it was possible to play.

Plenty of runs at club and school level meant my selection for the Pakistan Education Board and a first-class debut at the age of fourteen – young even for Pakistan where, because of the system, players tend to mature earlier than they do in England. The match was against

South Zone at Hyderabad. I was stumped for 0 in the first innings and 14 in the second and we lost the match by 114 runs. From an early age I learned to use my feet, but I still had to learn not to miss the ball in doing so. It was not the ideal start for a youngster looking to follow his brother's footsteps.

One of my contemporaries in that match was my former school captain, Mohammad Ilyas, who opened the innings and went on to play ten Test matches for Pakistan, opening the innings with the 'little master', Hanif Mohammad. Mohammad Ilyas's style of batting definitely influenced mine. He could cut and hook and was very strong off the back foot.

There are two first-class tournaments in Pakistan. The first is the Quaid-e-Azam Trophy, named after the founder of Pakistan, Mohammad Ali Jinnah, known as Quaid-e-Azam (Great Leader) and introduced in 1953/54 partly as an aid to selection of the team to tour England in 1954. It was comprised of teams representing regional cricket associations. The second is the Ayub Trophy, dating from 1960/61 and named after Ayub Khan, the second President of Pakistan. This provided competitive cricket for departmental sides such as those representing banks, railways, airlines and government departments. In later years it has become the BCCP Trophy, then the Patron's Trophy, then the President's Trophy.

In practice, however, the division between the two competitions has not always been clear cut and both have contained a mixture of regional and departmental teams. The Ayub Trophy has not always been first class and it has to an extent acted as a feeder to the senior league. In an attempt to provide teams of roughly equal strength, Karachi and Punjab each entered three teams from 1956/57 and at times Lahore has also produced two teams. Karachi provided the winner of seven consecutive tournaments. It is the largest city in Pakistan and had a population of around two million at the time. It is now around twenty-three million, the second largest in the world, after Shanghai.

There were some changes to the rules of the Quaid-e-Azam Trophy in that 1961/62 season. In an attempt to speed up the game, the first innings of a three-day match was restricted to four hours, of a four-day match to five and a half hours, and of a five-day match to seven hours. Furthermore, five bonus points were awarded to a side scoring at more than three runs per over and five for averaging twenty runs per wicket with an additional point for each over above an average of seventeen per hour. A new ball was available after fifty overs. It must have been a nightmare for captains who would be obliged to concentrate on matters other than simply winning the game. The general opinion was that the new rules were a success, but nevertheless they did not last very long.

In the Ayub Trophy, however, we did not have to bother with all that and it was there that, for the 1964/65 season, I played my cricket with the Education Board, captaining them in all the six matches in which I played. It was quite literally men against boys, but a great experience for boys seasoned in the competitive atmosphere of Pakistan schools cricket.

After that debut as a fourteen year old, I played no more first-class cricket for a couple of years until I was selected for the Lahore Whites against the Karachi Blues in the Quaid-e-Azam Trophy in March 1964. I was top scorer with 28 in a total of 113 in a match which we lost heavily on the first innings.

I began the 1964/65 season with an appearance for the BCCP XI against the Karachi Whites in a non-first-class match. Mohammad Ilyas was in the opposing team and scored a century. I didn't do quite as well as that, but still had 70 in the second innings. However, we lost the match by ten wickets. My first first-class century came for the Lahore Education Board in November 1964, 122 against Rawalpindi at the Pindi Club Ground in that city against a strong attack which included a couple of bowlers with Test experience, captain Munir Malik and Javed Akhtar, both of whom had toured England with Pakistan in 1962. I captained a young side who acquitted themselves pretty well against a team of more experienced cricketers.

We did not make the best of starts. I arrived at the crease with the scoreboard reading 16 for 2, soon afterwards to be 17 for 3 as my partner was run out for a duck. My next partner was Majid Khan (Majid Jahandir Khan as he was known then), just a year older than I was. We managed to put on 51 together before he fell, lbw to Javed Akhtar. Majid was soon to be a well-known figure on the national and international stage. He had already played the first of his sixty-three Test matches and he went on to distinguish himself in twenty-three one-day internationals, as well as with Glamorgan, Cambridge University and Queensland.

We eventually totalled 270 before Majid tore into the Rawalpindi top order to reduce them to 8 for 4. It was a beautiful spell. He swung the ball both ways at speed. They recovered from that position, but still could muster no more than 65, doing rather better in the follow-on reaching 172. I allowed myself three overs of left-arm spin, had a caught and bowled and took two other catches. Victory by an innings and 33 runs was a highly satisfactory outcome for us. We certainly lacked the experience of our opponents, but we were a talented and enthusiastic side, which went some way to restoring the balance. It was a very encouraging result and the press were very complimentary both about my own performance and the team's.

I continued to captain the Education Board side on their unbeaten run to the final. Against Peshawar University in a match reduced to two days, we had a convincing first-innings win, thanks to Majid's five for 32 reducing them to 82 all out. We then beat Combined Services by three wickets after being behind on the first innings, Majid top scoring in the first innings with 60 and I in the second with 57. A win on the first innings against Railways saw us into the semi-final against Pakistan International Airlines where Majid's 168 in a total of 527 meant an appearance in the final. That was a different story. We were walloped by an innings and 91 runs by a very strong Karachi side, but it was a privilege to be there and test ourselves against stronger opposition.

I finished the 1964/65 season playing for a combined Punjab University/Lahore Education Board side in the Quaid-e-Azam trophy. We were not out of our depth, drawing both matches, winning on the first innings against Lahore Reds and losing on the first innings against Railways.

It was an invaluable experience. Playing against the big boys in the fast lane was an eye-opener. My father always told us, when there was a discussion on cricket – a very frequent occurrence – 'You must try to play against strong opposition; it is harder to score runs, but they are runs that will mean much more to you than the runs you score against weaker bowling.'

Those ten matches were my early experience of first-class cricket in Pakistan. Two and a half years would pass before I played there again. Still aged only seventeen, I decided to try my luck in England. It was a decision instigated by and with the full support of my father and Saeed.

I was my brother's greatest fan and I took every opportunity to watch him, both in the nets and in the middle. I learned a lot. English cricket is covered in some detail in the Pakistani media and we all followed Surrey on the radio and in the newspapers with a sort of long-distance hero worship as they won the Championship in seven consecutive seasons. The names of Stuart Surridge, Peter May, Ken Barrington, Jim Laker, Tony Lock, Alec Bedser and Peter Loader were household names, as familiar to us as they were to any English cricket followers. My father used to keep scrapbooks of press cuttings of the great deeds of all the players. Fred Trueman was one of our heroes, particularly for his devastating performances against India and the astounding feat at the time of reaching 300 Test wickets. We scarcely believed it as we listened and read about Jim Laker taking nineteen wickets at Old Trafford in 1956. It was one of my father's dreams that one of his sons would play for Surrey, so Surrey would be my first port of call. If that didn't work, then there were fifteen other counties at which I might try my luck – it would be seventeen now, but Durham would not be on the scene for almost thirty years and Yorkshire still operated its native-born policy and continued to do so until Sachin Tendulkar became available.

There was a financial attraction to England too. There was no money in Pakistan cricket in those days. Players of exceptional talent were found 'employment' with Pakistan International Airlines or the Railways. That enabled them to play first-class cricket and get paid for it, though indirectly. The vast majority, however, were unpaid and played as amateurs. My schoolwork was above average, but at seventeen, I had no interest in any other job. I wanted to play cricket and had enough confidence in my own ability to believe I could do so professionally. Saeed and my father shared and encouraged my views. To try and make it in England was a no brainer.

One of the biggest influences on my career –
my brother Saeed, meeting the Queen during
the Lord's Test in 1987.

2

Through the Hobbs Gates

I landed at Heathrow on 22 April 1965. Saeed was contracted as professional to Nelson in the Lancashire League and would play for them that year and the following one. We flew over together from Karachi to London and were met at the airport by my brother Nasir. Saeed then transferred to a local flight to Manchester and I went to lodge with Nasir in New Malden. Nasir was studying for a degree in automobile engineering which would lead to a career with Volkswagen in Germany.

Nasir had been in the UK for three years and was well acclimatised. For me, it was the first time I had been out of Pakistan. Nasir was able to advise me on coping with the culture shock of switching from Lahore to south London, from an eastern way of life to a western one. They were two very different worlds. I was leaving behind a city where the mean temperature in April was around 27 degrees with highs of well over 30, trying to get used to a cold, damp English spring where the temperature was not much above freezing – or so it seemed. It was actually just into double figures. My native language is Urdu and, being from the Punjab, we also spoke Punjabi. English was my third language and, while I was reasonably competent, I now had to get used to it being spoken all the time – and with a south London accent as well. In early May I went with Nasir – also a good cricketer who could have played at first-class level had he not chosen to concentrate on his studies – to Malden Wanderers Cricket Club. We introduced ourselves and were made very welcome.

Saeed had played four matches with Surrey 2nd XI in 1964, having by that time played in a couple of dozen Test matches, so his pedigree was well established and his opinion respected. He arranged for me to have trials at The Oval – trials which consisted of having a fifteen-minute net under the close scrutiny of coach Arthur McIntyre and captain Micky Stewart.

It was an amazing experience. I stepped through the famous Hobbs Gates, aware that I was in a very special place: home of the first Test match in England, the ground which had given rise to the Ashes and, in traditionally hosting the last Test match of the summer, on several occasions the venue where the outcome of a series had been decided. It was where Jack Hobbs, Tom Hayward, Andy Sandham and Douglas Jardine had played their cricket. So many great names.

There I was, on the ground I had only read and heard about, in awe of the great team of the 1950s that had brought home seven consecutive Championship titles. It was an honour to bat and bowl in the same nets where so many of my heroes had practised before me, heroes like Peter May, Alec Bedser, Tony Lock, Jim Laker and Ken Barrington.

Nasir and I were shown to Arthur McIntyre's office and then to the junior dressing room where I was able to get changed, and from there to the nets at the Vauxhall End.

I was anxious to do well but very aware that conditions would be quite different to those I had grown up with at home. In Pakistan, where there is very little movement in the air or off the seam, it is usually safe to play straight balls through mid-wicket. Not so here where, especially in May, the ball swings and seams in a way I had not seen before.

I had telephoned Saeed the evening before and remembered his advice – head still, watch the ball and, above all, play straight. He had been one of the more successful members of a largely unsuccessful Pakistan side who had toured England under Javed Burki in 1962. He had scored 1,294 first-class runs at an average of 34.97 but Pakistan had lost the Test series 4-0 and won only one county match (ironically against Surrey, thanks in part to Saeed's second innings 108 not out). My brother was not alone in attributing the batting failures to an inability to adapt to English conditions. Until recently most pitches in Pakistan had been of matting, but the introduction of turf pitches meant virtually no deviation off the pitch and the atmosphere meant little swing in the air. Small wonder then that they were ill equipped to face the swing and seam bowling that English conditions encouraged.

I was faced with a barrage of quick and medium-pace swing and seam bowlers. Fifty years later, I can't remember who they were and I'm sure none of them will remember me either. Having survived that, I was then invited to bowl a bit of my left-arm spin and sent down a few fairly accurate ones. After that, I was informed that Mr McIntyre had called Nasir over and asked whether I would be available to play some 2nd XI cricket and Club and Ground matches when there was no 2nd XI match. We didn't need asking twice. I had come to play cricket... nothing else. He showed me round, then it was back to the upstairs dressing room where the junior players changed. The senior players had their own on the ground floor. Things have changed now, but there was a very clear hierarchy at this time and for many years afterwards.

Because of the requirement at the time to serve a two-year period of residence in the county, I played no Championship cricket before 1967 and was restricted to Club and Ground, 2nd XI and Colts matches. I also played for Malden Wanderers in the days before league cricket became widespread in the south of England, the Surrey Championship not getting off the ground until 1968. There was, however, far more cricket below 1st XI level and I was able to play most days of the week. I loved it and didn't let down either the club or myself.

The qualifying period did not prevent my playing in non-Championship matches and Surrey decided to give me a chance to play for the 1st XI in July against the touring South Africans. Usually, whether for training or a match for 2nd XI or Club and Ground, I travelled with my cricket bag from New Malden to Vauxhall station. This time, I was aware that the day was different. I normally shared the trains with commuters into the City, but they were more crowded that morning. I walked to The Oval from Vauxhall station surrounded by large numbers of people going to watch the cricket and arrived at the gate to be asked by the uniformed attendant where I thought I was going.

'To the dressing room,' I said.

'Not today you're not. There's a match on.'

'I know. I'm playing in it!'

'Not this one. There's a schools match in Kennington Park. Go and ask there – just the other side of the traffic lights. Now move out of the way and let the cars through. Come on, boy. Out of the way. This is a very busy day for me!'

I protested, but it made no difference. I was not going to be allowed into the ground. Eventually I was rescued by a committeeman in one of the cars I was supposed to let through. He recognised me and told the jobsworth to let me in. An hour later I was padding up to face Peter Pollock.

I made that debut for Surrey on 7 July 1965 at the age of 17 years and 260 days, at the time the seventh-youngest player to do so. I have since slipped to twelfth place, behind David Smith, Martin Bicknell, Alex Tudor and most recently Sam Curran. Tony Lock, at 17 years and 8 days remains top of the list.

The South Africans were a strong touring side. It was to be their last tour of England for more than thirty years. They would be ostracised from international cricket from 1969 as a result of the Nationalist Government's apartheid policy, an exile precipitated by the refusal to accept

Basil D'Oliveira as a member of the MCC touring party on the intended 1968/69 tour of the country.

All that, however, was in the future. In 1965 they had a powerful team with Peter van der Merwe as captain and future captain Ali Bacher in the squad, along with world-class players such as Eddie Barlow, Colin Bland, and Peter and Graeme Pollock.

Surrey fielded the strongest side they could. The glory days of the fifties were behind them, but under Micky Stewart they were a powerful outfit with Geoff Arnold and David Sydenham leading the attack, Arnold Long behind the stumps and Pat Pocock to provide the off spin, backed up by Stewart Storey, an extremely useful all-rounder.

With so many distinguished cricketers on both sides, I couldn't help feeling a little overawed, but I think I acquitted myself well enough, making 21 in the first innings before giving my wicket away to Peter Pollock and 66 in the second before getting out to off spinner Harry Bromfield. I had helped set up the third declaration with Stewart Storey in a rain-affected match which challenged the tourists to score 226 in just under three hours. Barlow had an impressive century in reply. It was the kind of closure to which in future years I was to become accustomed under the enterprising and courageous captaincy of Micky Stewart.

In his book written with Stephen Chalke, *Micky Stewart and the Changing Face of Cricket*, he remembers the occasion: 'A talented teenaged Pakistani, Younis Ahmed, arrived in 1965. He had to serve a two-year residential qualification before he could play in the Championship, but he had an outing in the first team when Surrey played the South Africans that July, showing the promise of his left-handed batting with scores of 21 and 66. "I was at the wicket when he came in," Micky recalls, "Even at that age he played in a very aggressive, confident way, looking to establish his ascendancy over the bowlers. He became a real match-winner. He could always score runs, all round the wicket, even when it was difficult.'"

It had been an amazing experience for me. On all three days the ground was packed, not an empty seat in the place. I was unused to such high-profile matches, but realised it was vitally important for me to perform well as the Surrey balcony was full of distinguished guests which included a number of former players, such as Stuart Surridge, Alec and Eric Bedser, Peter May, Jim Laker, Raman Subba Row and Alf Gover.

Also making his debut in that match was Ian Finlay, later to become my rival for a place in the side on the enforced retirement of Ken Barrington. He had a huge advantage over me at this time as, being Surrey-born, he was entitled to play in Championship matches, while I was serving my two-year qualification period. He opened with Micky Stewart but failed to reach double figures in either innings. Later he emigrated with his parents to South Africa where he played for South African Universities, Transvaal B, North Eastern Transvaal and Northern Transvaal.

In 1965 I had a fairly steady and satisfactory season with the 2nd XI, playing twenty-two matches and making 461 runs at an average of 27.11. I also bowled 110 overs and had eleven wickets at 21.45. In sixteen Club and Ground matches, I made 481 at an average of 43.72, as well as bowling 131.5 overs and taking twenty-five wickets at 13.8. Still only seventeen, I played a handful of matches for the Colts too. Overall, I wasn't too unhappy with my first season in England, feeling I had now got to grips with the climate and very different playing conditions.

Club and Ground matches are off the agenda now, but in their day they performed a couple of useful functions. Firstly, they provided match practice for those who were not playing regular 1st XI cricket and, secondly, they gave clubs and schools around the county the opportunity to step up to a higher standard and their players an opportunity to provide performances which might get them noticed. The Surrey Championship has taken over now to an extent, but the scouting system is a bit hit and miss. In recent years, Surrey have spent more time and money on overseas superstars than in scouring the county for longer-term talent. The Club and Ground fixtures are a link that has been lost and one wonders how many promising youngsters have slipped through the net.

There is nowhere in the world where conditions vary as much as they do in England. Later in my career I had to work to adjust my technique to bat on Australian, southern African and Caribbean pitches, but for the moment I was happy to have adjusted from the lifeless pitches and clear atmosphere of the subcontinent to the cloudy, swinging, seaming and sometimes spinning conditions of my adopted country.

It was Micky Stewart's benefit year and there was an opportunity to play in some benefit matches. These were social rather than competitive occasions, but I didn't mind that. More important than what happened on the field was the opportunity to meet, play with and, above all, learn from senior players such as Micky himself, Ken Barrington, Stewart Storey, John Edrich, Geoff Arnold and Arnold Long.

Despite my enjoyment of all the cricket I was able to play, it was frustrating not to be eligible for Championship matches, but I had no choice other than to accept it until I had completed my period of residence. With no experience of Championship cricket, I had no opportunity to absorb the atmosphere and bat against top-quality bowlers in the context of 1st XI competition before going out and facing someone like Peter Pollock in the occasional tour matches. It was like playing reserve team football, then being thrown into an international match.

The 2nd XI had a very good side in those days. Graham Roope and Robin Jackman, both to become international cricketers, were in the team, as was Derek Taylor, a high-class wicketkeeper who played regularly for Somerset throughout the 1970s and also played football for Corinthian Casuals. In 1966 we won the 2nd XI Championship. I remember Peter May coming into the dressing room to give us our medals. *Wisden* reported: 'Surrey, twelfth the previous year, won the Second Eleven Championship for the first time since it was inaugurated in 1959. Their success was largely a team effort with special emphasis on the captaincy of AJ McIntyre, the county coach. Mohammed Younis, a brother of Saeed Ahmed, the Pakistan Test player scored 1,048 runs, including three centuries and I Finlay also shone with the bat. DA Marriott bowled consistently well and DJS Taylor shone as wicketkeeper.'

I topped the batting averages with 1,048 runs at 47.63 with hundreds against Hampshire (169 not out at Guildford), Northamptonshire (132 not out at The Oval) and Glamorgan (104 at Newport). I also had 72 not out against Sussex at Guildford and, in a non-Championship match, 125 not out against the touring Western Province Willows. In other matches, I had 114 for the Club and Ground against Banstead and averaged 56 for the Colts, including 100 not out against Emanuel School.

As if playing for the 2nd XI and Club and Ground side were not enough, I played for the International Cavaliers. It was 40-over cricket on a Sunday afternoon televised on BBC 2 and the inspiration for the John Player League which began in 1969. It was at Saeed's instigation, my first match being against a Cambridge University Past and Present XI. There were also matches against the Oxford equivalent, most of the counties, who fielded full-strength sides, and a Rest of the World XI. The games were taken seriously. This was not Mickey Mouse cricket. There were some world-class cricketers in these teams and it was awesome to be sharing a dressing room with and playing against legends of the game such as Denis Compton, Ted Dexter, Godfrey Evans, Garry Sobers, the Pollock brothers, Bob Simpson, Graham McKenzie, Rohan Kanhai, Lance Gibbs, Saeed himself, Little Master Hanif, the Nawab of Pataudi and many others.

I learned a lot – especially from Garry Sobers, who was a very modest and approachable man, always willing to talk about the game and share his experiences. As a fellow member of the left-handers club, I was able to learn from his experience and benefit from his advice. To see how these great players approached the game was a unique experience and a huge privilege. I learned it was important not to give my wicket away, and once in to go and get three figures. Then, once there, why get out between 100 and 110? You're in and there's still time left. Why give it away? It was an attitude that remained with me. Looking at my list of centuries, I'm pleased to say that many were big ones.

I was selected to play for the Surrey 1st XI against the West Indies touring team. With all due respect to Banstead and Emanuel School, Charlie Griffith and Garry Sobers were going to be more of a challenge. Unfortunately rain prevented any play on the first two days, so a decision was taken to play a one-day match under the rules of the Gillette Cup, then still in its infancy but very popular with the public. Surrey had reached the final the previous year. First-class status was sacrificed as the match was restricted to sixty overs per innings and bowlers to ten overs each. The West Indians won easily, Surrey being able to manage only 188 for 9 despite Mike Edwards who batted through the innings for 108 not out. I was caught and bowled for 18 by Garry Sobers, who conceded a miserly thirteen runs from his ten overs. His opening partner, Charlie Griffith, who had terrified better batsmen than Surrey's lower middle order that season, ensured that few runs were added after I had left at 140 for 4. The tourists needed only forty-eight overs to reach their target.

It was a performance not untypical of the men from the Caribbean that summer. I followed with interest the England-West Indies Test series, won comfortably by the West Indies, but with a twist in the tail as, already 3-0 down in the series, the selectors brought back Brian Close as captain for the final Test at The Oval. He reduced the margin to 3-1, famously positioning himself at short leg to catch Sobers for a duck off John Snow. It was also Close who had engineered Yorkshire's win against Surrey in the previous year's Gillette Cup Final. In later years, he was to become one of my heroes.

I have often been asked whether I encountered any racism on my arrival in England. The straight answer is absolutely not, at least not on its cricket grounds and in its pavilions. We were all sportsmen and blind to variations of colour and creed. On the social scene it might have been different. Mass immigration from the Caribbean, beginning with the *Empire Windrush* in 1948, had occurred in the previous decade. It helped the UK economy by providing nurses and bus conductors and other low-paid jobs that were difficult to fill locally. Immigration from the subcontinent followed, Indians and Pakistanis providing much needed labour in the cotton and woollen mills of the north. The resident population became concerned that a cherished way of life was being threatened and the fears and suspicions were crystallised in Enoch Powell's 'rivers of blood' speech in 1968.

What I did encounter on the professional cricket scene was not so much racism as resentment that funds which might otherwise have been committed to the development of young, local talent was being diverted to usually well-paid overseas players at a time before the Test and County Cricket Board, a precursor of the ECB, restricted the number of overseas players on a county's books to two and then one.

There were three of my brothers in England. Saeed and Nasir I have already mentioned, but also Anwar, sadly no longer with us, who joined the MCC groundstaff a few years later and was around at the same time as Ian Botham. It came as no surprise to us that Anwar was involved in some high jinks with Botham. One day when it was raining and the young cricketers were confined to the dressing room, bored, larking about and looking for ways to amuse themselves and pass the time, a friendly dispute broke out between my brother and Ian about something quite trivial. It usually was with Anwar. On this occasion, the subject of the argument was the right of possession of a pint jug. Inevitably it broke, sending most of the glass into my brother's hand and creating a deep wound that required sixteen stitches. Both the protagonists were reprimanded – not for the first or only time in Botham's case, I guess. Anwar was unable to play cricket for about two months and obliged to take the role of scorer. On hearing of this, Saeed reckoned that's what he did best!

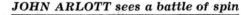

Surrey edge closer to Gloucester

In essence, because they are a balanced team, Surrey beat Sussex at The Oval yesterday and so moved to second position in the County Championship. After two slow-moving first innings, the last day and the match were resolved between the spin bowlers of the two teams.

Intikhab and Pocock, of Surrey, trusted and encouraged, made the utmost of a slow, turning wicket. Sussex, however, have long leaned heavily upon their fast bowlers and now, when their spin bowlers were offered opportunities, their craft had become dull. So Sussex were put out for 111 and Surrey scored 148 to win by four wickets.

Sussex showed an honest intent to score quickly and declare at the start of the morning when Tony Buss and Greig took runs at one a minute from Arnold and Jackson. They were reined in by Intikhab, who procured some wildly inaccurate guesses as to the direction of his breaks, and by Pocock, who flighted and turned his off-breaks. Greig hit Pocock firmly for Edrich to make a quick catch at silly mid-on, and when Pocock bowled Griffith through a cross-batted stroke, the Sussex innings lay open to destruction.

Tony Buss, unusually assured for an overnight stopgap, was the highest scorer, but he cannot have been surprised when at last a ball from Intikhab, which beat his stroke, also hit the stumps. Pocock had Parks firmly caught by Knight at deep mid-wicket from a pulled drive, and when Graves, who had alternated straight defence and horizontal sweeps, was bowled by Intikhab, Surrey had taken the morning.

Intikhab and Pocock, the one burly and phlegmatic, the other angular and eager, took one each of the remaining wickets and Surrey needed 148 to win in 165 minutes plus 20 overs.

In their quarter-hour before lunch, Tony Buss beat Edwards, who was lbw to a ball which moved late and sharply. Early in the afternoon, Knight, too, was lbw to Buss, then Edrich, shrewd and responsible, and Younis Ahmed, confident and aggressive, mounted the main stand of the innings.

Lewis does not have the long and regular bowling spells which would give him confidence in his variety and tactics, while Cooper, given nine overs last season, must almost have forgotten that he was once regarded as an all-rounder. They both spun and turned, but not with full control and assurance.

Younis hit two sixes and nine fours in little over an hour, but Edrich broke his flow when he drove almost casually to Hone, the substitute for Lenham, at mid-off. Younis was caught by Greig, stretching himself horizontally to his full and considerable length at short mid-off, and Surrey went to tea at 120 for four, needing another 28 to win, and without anxiety.

Within a quarter of an hour afterwards, both Roope and Smith were caught at the wicket from ill-judged strokes against Lewis and, at 123 for six, Surrey, for the first time, could doubt their ability to win. Intikhab, however, revealing yet another facet of his value, settled with massive calm, easing the atmosphere and steadying both the innings and his partner, Long. Lewis bowled his utmost but, a few minutes after five o'clock, Intikhab heaved Cooper for a straight six and, within moments, the matter was settled according to form.

SUSSEX.—First innings 276 (M. Buss 111, L. J. Lenham 51 ; G. Arnold 5 for 52).
SURREY.—First innings 234 for 9 den. (A. Buss 4 for 59).
SUSSEX—Second innings
(Overnight 26 for 3)
A. Buss b Intikhab 38
A. W. Greig c Edrich b Pocock 15
M. G. Griffith b Pocock 7
P. J. Graves b Intikhab 14

Starting to draw attention to myself –
John Arlott praises me in the press.

3

First XI Regular

I played fairly regularly in 1967 and 1968, gaining experience and adjusting my technique to be successful as
a contracted player in English conditions. Players from
the subcontinent specialise in working the middle stump
ball through mid-wicket and mid-on, but I had to curtail
my natural instinct to play those strokes, a risky practice
in England where pitches are greener and county attacks
are dominated by fast and medium-pace bowlers specialis-
ing in moving the ball both in the air and off the seam.
I had learned before my first net that I had to play a lot
straighter and play the ball as late as possible, techniques
which I continued to put into practice.

The Surrey coach, Arthur McIntyre, was a hard and
strict man who would certainly make his views known to
any player he felt had got himself out. There were a number of occasions in 1966 and 1967 when I was subjected
to some pretty tough talking and I knew that in the next

innings I must cut out any risky shots. It was hard at the time, but in the long run the lectures were of enormous help, repeating the lessons taught by my father on the value of concentration and playing long innings.

Two big influences in those early years were Micky Stewart and Ken Barrington, both very approachable and always willing to advise and share the benefit of their experience. Micky was always quick to congratulate 2nd XI players who had done well. He was a motivator, an important part of man management. Micky had modelled himself on his predecessor, Stuart Surridge, in that he had a plan for each batsman and pursued it ruthlessly. Against Keith Fletcher of Essex, for instance, who was strong off the back foot and excelled in the cut shot, the instructions were not to bowl short outside off stump and any bowler failing to follow those instructions, whether novice or established Test performer, was certain to receive the sharp side of the captain's tongue.

In those less democratic days, capped and uncapped players had separate dressing rooms, a relic and distortion of the days of Gentlemen and Players when amateurs and professionals were similarly separated and treated quite differently by county committees. The distinction was abolished in the early sixties, though separate dressing rooms for capped and uncapped players continued at The Oval for thirty years after that until Australian David Gilbert, astonished that such distinctions could still exist, followed the example of Berlin a few years earlier and ordered the demolition of the wall. In my day, however, it was still the practice that junior players contacted the senior ones by knocking on the door and asking for permission to enter the changing room.

I started the 1967 season with four 2nd XI matches and did enough to be given a Championship debut against Hampshire at Basingstoke. It was not the best of starts, lbw to Bob Cottam for a duck, but I did a bit better in the second innings with 26 not out and for the remainder of that season was able to hold a regular 1st XI place.

The Club Yearbook for 1968 mentions that Younis, Finlay and Smith all batted well at times. I was pretty pleased with my performances. Of my 83 against Leicestershire at Grace Road, *Wisden* said, 'A subsequent decline was halted by Younis the Pakistan batsman, who hit ten boundaries and played delightfully off the back foot in a seventh-wicket partnership with Long.'

Later in the season I had my first century for the county (of the nineteen I was to make over this and the following eleven seasons) against Derbyshire at The Oval, a score of 103 which helped Surrey to a first-innings lead with eighteen fours 'in a dashing display' according to *Wisden*.

Although I made little contribution in the following match, it was an incredible game of cricket. At 16 for 7, following Sussex's 163 all out at Hove, we were in deep trouble as John Snow and Tony Buss demolished the top order. However, a spirited partnership from Graham Roope and Arnold Long brought us back into the match and restricted Sussex's first innings lead to 48. Tidy bowling and fielding meant a target of 195 in four hours on a rain-affected pitch. It would have to be the highest innings of the match – and with steady innings from Mike Edwards and Bill Smith, we made it; Graham and Arnold at the crease again with four wickets and seventeen balls to spare. In practice it was three wickets in hand as David Gibson had, in pre-helmet days, been whisked off to hospital having been struck on the head by a Snow bouncer.

A wet August saw draws against Middlesex, Essex and Nottinghamshire, but we had done enough to secure fourth place in the Championship behind Yorkshire, Kent and Leicestershire.

There were twin tours in 1967 by teams from the subcontinent. Surrey had a comprehensive victory by eight wickets over an Indian side which included the spin trio of Chandrasekhar, Prasanna and Bedi. John Edrich and Ken Barrington led the way with 108 and 84 respectively. I made only 25 before Bedi had me lbw, but it was a privilege and an experience to be playing against such a distinguished side. Farokh Engineer in the first innings and Hanumant Singh in the second took the batting honours for India while our match winner was Pat Pocock with nine wickets for 119 in the match.

Playing against the Pakistan touring team in 1967 was a special experience for me. I did not distinguish myself in a drawn match, being caught and bowled by Hanif Mohammad for 6 as Ian Finlay held the innings together with a century, but it was a pleasure to be able to play against my brother, Hanif and my old friend Mohammad Ilyas. Unfortunately Ilyas, who had opened the innings with Javed Burki, twisted his ankle while going for a second run, retired hurt for 27 and did not play for another three weeks. In terms of averages, although I came nowhere near the 40-plus of Barrington, Edrich and Stewart, I thought I had reason to feel satisfied with my first Championship season.

Sunday was still a non-match day and I managed a handful of International Cavaliers matches including one against a star-studded Rest of the World XI at Ascott Park in Wing.

At the end of the 1967 season I returned to Pakistan and played in three first-class matches, firstly for Pakistan against The Rest at Sahiwal. The match was drawn. Hanif captained and the batting order was a little eccentric. I opened (not my usual position, at least in first-class matches) with Saeed at number three and Hanif at number five. I had 41 in the first innings and top scored with 58 in the second. I then played for Karachi against Railways in the final of the Quaid-e-Azam Trophy (left over from the previous season) at the National Stadium. We won by ten wickets, my contribution being negligible in a total of 572. Asif Ahmed and Saeed both had hundreds, while Intikhab Alam was the main destroyer with six wickets in the first innings. Saeed also chipped in with five in the match. Finally I played, also with Saeed, in a non-competition match for the Khairpur Commissioner's XI and the Public Works Department. It was a low-key affair, ending as a draw. Most people had a bowl. I opened the batting and sent down a few expensive overs.

Fenner's and The Parks the following May were something of a contrast. After an indifferent start to the season, I found myself in the 2nd XI for a while, but bounced back with 136 not out against Middlesex at Norbury. It was about this time I changed my name from Mohammad Younis to Younis Ahmed. Our family tradition was that names were chosen by grandparents, but Pakistani names can be a nightmare for genealogists as they are often different from those of either parent and it is not always easy to establish a family link. People would say to me, 'How can you be Saeed Ahmed's brother with a name like Mohammad Younis?' So I took the decision to change and come into line with western practice, as many families, particularly those settled in the UK, tend to do nowadays. It cemented a closer family link between Saeed and myself.

My average the following year improved to the extent that I was second to John Edrich, but for the county it was not a good season. They finished fifteenth in the Championship, Edrich scoring the solitary Championship century. *Wisden* was sympathetic to the situation in which I found myself, stating that too much was left to be done by the less experienced batsmen and mentioning that Graham Roope and I made encouraging progress.

After my brief sojourn with the 2nd XI, I consolidated my place with a half century against Kent at Blackheath, then 96 against Sussex at Hove. Part of the half century was against 'declaration' bowling, as Kent were more interested in a target being set rather than bowling us out. The plan backfired as Stewart Storey and Roger Harman cleaned up our hosts for 86, leaving Surrey winners by 83 runs, a result scarcely anticipated when we were more than a hundred behind on first innings. My effort at Hove was more of a proper knock. *Wisden* commended my 'adventurous spirit' as I hit eleven fours. Another one would have given me a century, but a reasonable total was assured. It was still not enough as Sussex then took a lead of

112, but a good batting surface and a long rain break on the last day put paid to any chance of a result.

I was back in the 2nd XI for a brief spell in August, even managing to take the wickets of both openers in a dead match against Warwickshire at The Oval. Otherwise I did little of note, but no one else was performing either, so by the middle of the month I was in the 1st XI and played no more 2nd XI cricket for another six years.

A number of poor team batting performances followed. There were a few rain-affected draws, then a dreadful spell of three defeats on the trot, away to Glamorgan, Northamptonshire and Yorkshire. It was the last of these that saw my first encounter with the blood and guts approach of Brian Close, who was to play a large part in my later career. He had taken over the captaincy of Yorkshire in 1963 and was on the verge of leading them to their seventh Championship in ten seasons. They had dominated the sixties in the way Surrey had the fifties and towards the end of the season we played them at Hull, a ground no longer used for first-class cricket, in a match which would give the Yorkies the title if they won it. Surrey were never in a winning position, but on the third evening we were in with a good chance of salvaging a draw. Yorkshire's left-arm spinner, Don Wilson, who, in the match went through 100 wickets in first-class matches and 700 Championship wickets in his career, relates in Stephen Chalke's *Caught in the Memory: County Cricket in the 1960s*: 'Younis Ahmed batting magnificently and only ten minutes to go ... Then Younis plays a full-blooded sweep off Don Wilson that ricochets off Brian Close at silly short-leg and is caught by Jimmy Binks. "There was blood everywhere," Don recalls, "but Closey wouldn't go off. It's in the mind, this pain, he said. He was absolutely mental.'"

Shortly afterwards, Pat Pocock was run out, Robin Jackman lbw and Yorkshire were champions again.

There were a couple of matches for the International Cavaliers that summer and two for Surrey against them. In the first at Cheam, Saeed playing for the opposition had a duck, while I scored 10. Bragging rights to Younis. And in the second, at The Oval for John Edrich's benefit, Saeed had 9. Then it rained, saving him from a whitewash over the summer.

Ill-health had compelled Ken Barrington to retire before the start of the 1969 season, after he suffered a heart attack during a benefit match in Australia. I remember very clearly the announcement on the nine o'clock news. Surrey and England were deprived of a world-class batsman, but it did give me the opportunity to cement a place in Ken's spot at number four.

Micky was very up front about the situation when we reported back to The Oval on 1 April. Everyone was very sorry about Ken of course – it was a great loss for Surrey and England. He had produced brilliant performances on the field and was well respected off it. But life goes on – as does cricket – and there was an opportunity for someone to fill Ken's shoes. He had one or two people in mind and they would be given an opportunity, not just in one match but in three or four. After my performances in the previous season I reckoned I had a good chance, rose to the challenge, scored a few runs, took the vacant place and, barring injuries, would be virtually an automatic selection for the next few seasons.

It was my best summer for Surrey. I was the first to 1,000 first-class runs, had 1,760 in all at 47.56 with five centuries, the first four of which were not out. The Yearbook was complimentary: 'Batting or fielding, Surrey could always be relied upon to entertain and on most occasions did so. John Edrich, Michael Edwards and Micky Stewart led the way and were splendidly supported by Younis Ahmed and Graham Roope – who both won caps.'

The Yearbook also recognised the role played by Arthur McIntyre, and there was perhaps something in that. It would be an exaggeration to say that the 2nd XI which won the 2nd XI Championship in 1966 was the same players who would go on to win the 1st XI Championship in 1971, but there were common elements – Geoff Arnold and Robin Jackman among the bowlers, and Graham Roope and myself among the batters. For 1969, Surrey had a well-balanced team. It fell away a bit at the end and we finished third, but it was the best for several seasons.

Facing the West Indies at The Oval in 1969 was an interesting and challenging experience. It was not quite the four-pronged pace attack that Clive Lloyd was later to have at his disposal, but it was still quite useful and not exactly slow. It comprised Philbert Blair and Grayson Shillingford followed up by Charles Davis and Garfield Sobers – although he bowled left-arm spin on this occasion. I arrived at the crease after Bill Smith had been hit on the head by Shillingford. Bill had shaped to hook a short ball – and missed it. The ball had smashed into his nose. There were no helmets then and a cricket ball hitting you at around ninety miles per hour is going to make a big mess. Bill was down on the ground, blood everywhere. David Montague, our popular physio known as Monty, rushed on with towel and spray. That was never going to be enough. Bill was carried from the field half-conscious. I was next in. I arrived at the crease to find a worrying mixture of blood and sawdust. Game on!

The first ball to me was – inevitably – a bouncer. So was the next. I reminded the bowler that he was allowed to put it in my half of the pitch. It made no difference, so after that, I was ready on the back foot and hooked him for four. My partner Graham Roope adopted similar tactics, and we tamed the attack to an extent and put on 105 for the second wicket. We were eventually able to declare with a lead of 184 and if rain had not washed out the final day, we may very well have gone on to win the match.

Wisden was very complimentary, saying, 'Younis had a splendid season, playing attractive, enterprising cricket in all circumstances. He and his fellow Pakistani, Intikhab, contributed aggression, which did much to lift the side from the previous summer's depression.'

I was that year the county's leading run scorer in first-class cricket, as indeed I would be for six out of seven seasons, including one where I shared top position with Graham Roope.

1969 saw an innovation whose far-reaching repercussions were scarcely appreciated at the time. Based on the hugely successful and popular International Cavaliers matches, the John Player League was launched. No coloured clothing or powerplays back then; the matches were meant to be fun and take the game to grounds which did not normally host county cricket. The Gillette Cup, ini-

tially 65 overs, then 60, had been tentatively introduced
in 1963. Originally known as simply the 'new knockout
competition', it attracted huge crowds, 25,000 at Lord's
finals. But the Cavaliers had demonstrated that that there
was an appetite for a shorter form of the game which could
be played on a league basis, thus ensuring that there were
opportunities to watch limited overs cricket regularly, not
just once or twice until the county supported went out of
the cup. These matches could be squeezed into an afternoon and evening after lunch on Sundays. The availabil-
ity of a beer tent at a time when, under more restrictive
licensing laws than today, pubs were closed, proved an
additional attraction. Changing leisure patterns, shorter
attention spans and recovery from the post-war austerity
of the 1950s doubtless also played their part and a third
limited overs competition – the Benson and Hedges Cup
combining mini-league and knockout formats – hit the
county scene in 1972. The balance between three-day and
one-day cricket was changing. A year earlier the first limited overs international was played when heavy rain caused
the Melbourne Test match to be abandoned without a
ball bowled and a one-day match was substituted. It did
not take long for this small spark to become a raging fire.

Coincidentally, Surrey's second match in the new competition, against Derbyshire, was played literally a cricket
ball's throw from where I currently live, on the ground
of Sutton Cricket Club in Cheam Road. A later match
was played at St John's School in Leatherhead. Otherwise
matches were at The (then unsponsored) Oval and, like
Twenty20 later, tended to be allocated there when the

possibility of increased gate receipts and bar profits sent the pound signs flashing in administrators' eyes.

Despite having a good season in the first-class game, I did nothing spectacular in the new competition, not getting past 50 in fifteen innings, though I did have 54 in the Gillette Cup match against Hampshire. Future years would be better.

Regular 40-over cricket was new to everyone and there was some feeling that 50 or 60 overs would make for a better competition – the Gillette Cup was 60 overs at the time. But the spectator appeal was undeniable, 40-over cricket put bums on seats that remained empty during the week and for many counties brought some relief to a parlous financial situation. It was also part of the beginnings of sponsorship, which soon was to become an invaluable and lucrative part of the game. In some cases it came to be too successful. Gillette pulled out a few years later when the public began to associate its name with cricket rather than razor blades.

It was during that season that I was awarded my county cap, along with Intikhab, Graham Roope and Derek Taylor. Being awarded a county cap is a significant moment in the career of any young player, indicating that in cricket terms he has come of age and is recognised as a regular member of the squad with something to contribute. Not that there was always an opportunity to do that. Despite my being capped I still remained a junior player. Yes, there were team meetings; when things had not gone right on the field they often went on for two or three hours, but generally it was a sell-and-tell approach. The captain and coach had their opinions, made the decisions and con-

veyed them and while there might be discussions within
an inner coterie of senior players, there was no wholesale
or widespread consultation or democracy. The opinions
of junior players were neither sought nor given and it was
not for a further three years or so, around 1972 after half
a dozen seasons of 1st XI cricket, that I began to be considered (and consider myself) a senior player.

Being awarded my cap made a huge difference to me
financially. As a 2nd XI and uncapped player, I was on a
very much hand-to-mouth existence and had to watch
every penny. Now, I was a lot more secure and was able to
afford and enjoy what had previously been out-of-reach
luxuries like meals in restaurants.

I wore that cap with pride as, with Mike Edwards, I
shared a partnership of over 200 in the second innings
against Gloucestershire at The Oval in June to enable
Micky Stewart to declare. Intikhab, with six for 29, set
up a 213-run victory which took Surrey to the top of the
table. On my innings, John Mason in the *Daily Telegraph*
reported: 'At present Younis must find this game quite the
easiest ever devised by man. His 113 was his fourth hundred of the season, all of which have been not out, and his
second against Gloucestershire in a week. That very new
county cap was at a jaunty angle.'

The following year's *Wisden* was also complimentary:
'Between these innings [Gloucestershire's 158 and 92]
Surrey had shown their batting might during a stand of
203 between Edwards and Younis. Younis, again in devastating stroke making form, reached his hundred with
fourteen fours in two and three-quarter hours. Edwards,

who was also in excellent form, batted an hour longer and hit thirteen fours.'

The other innings to which John Mason refers was 122 not out the previous week at Bristol, against an attack which, like that I faced at The Oval, included Mike Procter and spinners John Mortimore and David Allen, not the worst in the world, and one which took Gloucestershire to a podium finish of second behind Glamorgan.

Matches against Yorkshire were always a challenge I enjoyed. We were drawn against them at The Oval in the quarter-final of the Gillette Cup. It was a beautiful day and a good batting pitch and I was looking forward to the opportunity to get Surrey into the semi-finals. Thanks mainly to a partnership of over 150 between Geoffrey Boycott and Close – Boycs anchoring one end and Closey playing strokes at the other – Yorkshire built up a total of 272, very respectable in those days. Despite the loss of two early wickets I was confident we could do it. Chris Old, however, had other ideas. When he was fully fit – which, admittedly, was not often – Chris was a very fine bowler, swinging the new ball both ways at speed. He also had a very effective bouncer, as I was to discover to my cost. Having swung a couple each way at me, he let his bouncer go. An important part of the art of batting is to pick the length early and get into position. On this occasion I did just that but misjudged the pace. The ball crashed into the side of my head. My new cap offered me a little protection, but helmets were still a thing of the future. 'Retired hurt 0' was the forlorn scorecard entry. Unsurprisingly, I remember nothing about the rest of the match, but there was no way back. Surrey collapsed to lose by 138 runs and Yorkshire went on to win the cup.

My friend Mohammad Iqbal played some 2nd XI cricket that year, making 540 runs at an average of 30 with a highest score of 109. Outside the county circuit, I played for the Cricketers Association in a friendly at Driffield. My form of the summer continued. Most players on both sides had a bowl. I was one of the few that did not, but was quite happy with my 96. Test cricket would soon be coming up. After the summer I had had, I was ready for it, if perhaps not for the pitches we would play on.

It was during the 1969 season that I first met Gloria, who was later to become my wife. She was one of a group of four Australian girls who were 'doing Europe' and had got as far as London. One of them was a friend of Graham McKenzie of Western Australia, who was at the time playing for Leicestershire, and had arranged tickets for them for the John Player League match at The Oval. Apparently I was admired from afar, though at first she thought I was Greek. I doubt whether it was my batting she admired as I was stumped by Roger Tolchard off Jack Birkenshaw for just a single.

After the match we adjourned to the Surrey Tavern – now sadly demolished – where Graham approached and said there was someone who would like to meet me. I was introduced to Gloria and her friends. We chatted pleasantly and during the course of the conversation it emerged that it was Gloria's birthday the following day. There was to be a party. Would I like to go? Can a duck swim? Blonde and sun-tanned, Gloria was a very attractive, typically Australian girl.

There developed a very close relationship. Gloria decided to stay in England, finding employment first with Revlon and then with Estée Lauder working at Selfridge's and Harrod's.

It was also around this time that, through a mutual friend, I had the great privilege of having dinner with Richard Burton and Elizabeth Taylor. Recently married, they were staying at the Dorchester Hotel on Park Lane and working on an adaptation of Shakespeare's *The Taming of the Shrew*. We met at a restaurant in South Kensington where I found them to be a delightful and entertaining couple with a wonderful range of anecdotes. One I particularly remember was how, before one of the volatile scenes between Petruchio and Katherina, it was decided a couple of drinks would help. Elizabeth duly had her two and Richard had rather more, with the result that the shooting of the scene had to be delayed by several hours. Peter Sellers was also part of our group. He was to become a loyal friend, always willing to listen. He was one of the funniest men I have ever met, telling jokes with a perfectly straight face, never laughing at his own. Only if asked would he talk about himself.

Pakistan International Airlines, winners of
the Quaid-e-Azam Trophy in 1969.
I'm standing on the far left, my fellow debutant
Zaheer Abbas is kneeling, second from right.

4

Under the National Flag

As a consequence of my successful 1969 season, I was beginning to be spoken of as a possible England player. I
had lived in the country long enough to be qualified by
residence and was very much in the mind of Alec Bedser,
Chairman of Selectors. As it happened, the planned tour
of England by South Africa in 1970 never took place, the
beginnings of a more than twenty-year sporting boycott
of that country because of apartheid. It was replaced by
a series of matches against the Rest of the World, considered to be and advertised as Test matches at the time – a
status subsequently withdrawn.

More significant for me, however, was the impending
Pakistan tour of England in 1971. My parents were living
in Wimbledon at the time. Saeed was likely to play for
Pakistan and my father in particular was unhappy that his
sons should appear on opposite sides in a Test match. It
was a family decision, taken after long deliberation, that I

should focus on playing my international cricket for Pakistan.

It has been suggested that I had been invited and declined to play in the 1968/69 Pakistan-England series, a hastily arranged tour to replace England's one to South Africa, from which they withdrew as a result of the South African government's declining to accept Basil D'Oliveira as a member. I am not sure where that suggestion came from. In later years I was to turn down an invitation to represent my country because of earlier contractual commitments, but who, at the age of twenty-one and without good reason, turns down an opportunity to make a Test debut? Sure, the fee was nothing to write home about and there may well have been financial sacrifices to make, but travel and accommodation expenses would be met and, as in many other professions, it is sometimes necessary to accept less than ideal conditions in order to get on the ladder and climb to a better deal later on.

That invitation never occurred, but after five years in England with just a brief return to Pakistan in late 1967 when I played three first-class matches, I found myself flying back to my homeland. Eleven days after the final county match of the season, I was playing for Pakistan International Airlines in the semi-final and final of the Quaid-e-Azam Trophy. I needed to re-acclimatise to subcontinental conditions ahead of my Test match debut against New Zealand at the National Stadium in Karachi.

My belief was that I would play all three matches in the series of four-day Tests, using the PIA matches as warmups. Unfortunately that did not happen, but I was nevertheless extremely proud and greatly honoured to have the opportunity to represent my country.

At the time cricketers were not well paid; those from Pakistan even less so. There are stories that in the early days like the 1954 tour of England, some players from poorer backgrounds were reduced to borrowing boots and other items from friends and fellow players. Things had improved a little by the sixties and seventies, but the operation was still unprofessional. Maybe I was ahead of my time in suggesting that the PCB should pay players properly for doing a proper job of work. We have moved on since then to the extent that now Pakistan has followed the example of England, Australia and other countries in awarding central contracts to the top thirty or so players.

My debut was shared with off-spinner Mohammad Nazir and Zaheer Abbas, who batted at five. His eight first-class centuries had earned him selection. Sadiq Mohammad was another debutant – it was only the third occasion in the history of Test cricket that three brothers had played in the same team, Sadiq joining Hanif and Mushtaq. I batted at three in the first innings, splitting the three brothers, on a minefield of a pitch.

The plan to prepare such a bad pitch was that of Abdul Hafeez Kardar, who had captained Pakistan on their initial tour of England in 1954 and who now exercised a dictatorial domination of Pakistan cricket, later becoming President of the Pakistan Cricket Board. It was a pitch totally unworthy of a Test match, beginning to turn from the fifth over and from which, as *Wisden* correctly reported, pieces were cut regularly by almost every ball.

Left-arm spinner Hedley Howarth was soon operating and Pakistan were quickly in trouble, losing a number of wickets cheaply. I was out to Howarth for eight, fending off a ball which rose from a length and took the gloves to have me caught at short leg.

My Surrey colleague Intikhab Alam was captain. Initially it was to have been my brother Saeed, but a disagreement with Kardar led to his removal, not only as captain, but from the whole series. The expectation was that Intikhab's leg spin would bowl out New Zealand cheaply. It did not happen. Saeed's experience and all-round ability was missed. He was not only an outstanding batsman, but had also developed into a very fine off spinner. Mohammad Nazir bowled beautifully, but despite his seven for 99, the visitors built a first innings lead of 54

I did rather better in the second innings, batting at five and top scoring with 62, enabling Intikhab to declare, setting New Zealand 230 to win in three and a quarter hours. They ended on 112 for 5, but it was overall an unsatisfactory match.

Zaheer Abbas was subsequently dropped from the team after just one game; it turned out to be Hanif Mohammad's last Test. That decision was also taken by AH Kardar.

Despite his magnificent career, Hanif – the Little Master – was denied the send off that his many worshippers would have loved. He was a phenomenal player who had served Pakistan superbly, playing in fifty-five out of Pakistan's first fifty-seven matches. His sixteen-hour plus 337 in 1958/59 against the West Indies in Barbados and his world record (at the time) of 499 run out indicate the level of his skill and ability to play long innings. He was still only thirty-four, and in his own judgment, still able to play at top level for another three or four years. Like Saeed, he had been Kardar's find; like Saeed too, he was sidelined by the same man.

Says Peter Oborne, 'Such was the end of one of Pakistan's greatest players. As long as test cricket is played, Hanif's patience, single-mindedness, dedication, raw courage and extraordinary powers of concentration will always be marvelled at and celebrated.' Regrettably, Hanif's departure from the international scene was less glamorous than his batting had been. It is hard to digest, but it is not the only instance of Kardar's influence.

Kardar dominated Pakistan cricket for more than a quarter of a century, from the birth of the country in 1947 until 1975 when he crossed swords with an even more powerful despot in the form of President Zulfikar Ali Bhutto. Politics and cricket are inextricably linked in Pakistan. Constitutionally the President of the country is Patron of the Pakistan Cricket Board. That is not the same relationship as, say, Her Majesty the Queen being Patron of Surrey County Cricket Club. In Pakistan, the position of Patron is not just a figurehead or a name on the notepaper. Presidents can and do take an active interest in the cricket and intervene when they feel they need to. Thus, the power struggles of politics are reflected in abrupt changes of leadership in the administration of cricket. Aware of this and a supporter of PPP (Pakistan People's Party), Kardar always carried with him in the pocket of one of his expensive suits an undated but signed letter of resignation.

Osman Saliuddin has described Abdul Hafeez Kardar as an absolute monarch. He relates the story of a player who asked to be rested from a particular match. Kardar agreed but made him twelfth man and told him to tidy up the dressing room. When the player refused, he was dropped from the team for the next Test match, despite Kardar's having been responsible for his initial selection. Further anecdotal evidence is a story of a batsman who, having been reprimanded for a careless stroke, made a flippant remark and was never invited to play Test cricket again. I have no idea whether these stories are true, but they are consistent with the AH Kardar I knew. They are demonstrations of the man's ability to make and break a career, and also of his capacity to make cricket decisions for non-cricketing reasons. There is no doubt that the Oxford-educated Kardar was an intellectual man who played a huge part both pre- and post-partition in putting Pakistan cricket on the map and preventing it from being merely an offshoot of the Indian game. But he could be cruel and heartless, capable of destroying lives and careers and not hesitating to do so.

Kardar was a strong personality who was reluctant to admit that there was room for any opinion beyond his own. There was already ample evidence to support Kardar's reputation as a control freak and there would be more in future years. My brother Saeed always had a tremendous regard for the man who was his first international captain on the tour of West Indies in 1957/58. My own relationship with him turned out to be less smooth. During the first Test, I did not manage to have any interesting or constructive conversations with him, although I was eager to listen and learn from his vast experience.

From Karachi we moved on to my home town of Lahore. From the newspapers, it was apparent that there was much unhappiness about the omission of Hanif, and to a lesser extent of Zaheer Abbas. Not that this deterred Kardar, who had a hide like a rhinoceros and was impervious to criticism.

New Zealand, at the time the lowest ranked of the Test-playing nations, won the second Test in Lahore by five wickets, their first win against Pakistan. I was bowled by Dayle Hadlee for a duck – I was not alone in that – and made 19 in the second innings. After that defeat, more heads had to roll. Mine was one of them, along with those of Salahuddin and Mushtaq Mohammad. We were omitted for the final Test in Dacca in East Pakistan (now Bangladesh).

I was disappointed. International selection is a privilege accorded to very few cricketers and while no one has a divine right to it – as amply demonstrated by the Hanif Mohammad case – I felt after my successful season in county cricket in England the previous summer, I deserved another go. Even if I were not to be selected, it would not have been impossible to include me in the squad of players to travel to Dacca so that I could continue to absorb the Test match atmosphere and psychologically feel part of Pakistan's cricketing future. I felt the Chairman of Selectors should have explained to me why I had not been selected, not even to travel, and also asked if I'd had any problems with my teammates. I hadn't, but it would have been good practice to raise the question.

It did not happen. I played no more Test cricket for more than seventeen years.

The last match was drawn, brought to a premature conclusion by a riot, giving New Zealand their first ever series win in forty years as a Test-playing nation. Rioting was unfortunately becoming a feature of subcontinent cricket, only one of the three Test matches on England's tour of the previous year having escaped it. Visitors to Pakistan soon came to appreciate that rioting, which can sometimes spill over into violence, was part of the scene in Pakistan; rubber bullets, truncheons and tear gas are part of police armoury. The one riot-free match was in Dacca where crowd control was supervised by student leaders, rather than police or the army. Maybe there is a lesson there.

Although the Test series was disappointing, both for Pakistan and myself, I did manage a bit of success in domestic cricket that season. I was contracted to Pakistan International Airlines, using the semi-final and final of the Quaid-e-Azam Trophy against Karachi Whites and then the Public Works Department as a warm up for the Tests matches. In the first of these we had a comfortable win on first innings, my single figure score being bookended by centuries from Hanif, Mohammad Ilyas, Mushtaq and Zaheer Abbas. We won the final by 195 runs but Saeed, who was in the Public Works Department team, reclaimed the bragging rights he had surrendered in the Surrey-International Cavaliers match at The Oval earlier in the year, catching me in the first innings and having me caught by Aftab Baloch in the second in a spell of five for 80.

I stayed on in Pakistan after the Test matches, playing in the Ayub Trophy for Pakistan International Airlines A. In the group stage, we had comfortable wins against Lahore Blues and Punjab University. In the first of these I was run out for 99. I needed to stay in as wickets were falling at the other end. Mohammad Ilyas, Zaheer Abbas, Hanif and Mushtaq were all back in the hutch without having made much of a contribution. I was at the non-striker's end when Wasim Bari, a great wicketkeeper but indifferent judge of a run, called me for a single and then changed his mind, leaving me stranded in the middle of the pitch. It was a classic 'yes... no... sorry' situation.

However, I compensated for that in the second of the final matches with 147 not out, my highest first-class score to date. I arrived at the crease at 207 for 5 and enabled the team, captained by Hanif, to declare on 459 for 6, Hanif himself having contributed 113. Hanif, now released from Test responsibilities, played with freedom and did so again in the next match with 190 which saw us to a trophy-winning total of 561. Mushtaq supported him with 123. There was, however, some turgid cricket at times. The innings lasted for 240 overs, Hanif occupying the crease for just over nine hours, Mushtaq for four and a half. Zaheer Abbas will remember the match for another reason – out after hitting the ball twice for no score.

As well as recording my highest innings that season, I also produced my best bowling figures of three for 12 for The Rest v Pakistan at Sahiwal, but in fairness to bowlers of a more full-time nature, my victims were the last three batsmen!

In late January and early February I had a break from competitive cricket and met up again with the International Cavaliers for a brief tour of Jamaica. It came at a good time for me after the disappointment of being omitted from the Test team. The camaraderie in the Cavaliers team had always been of the best, but the advent of the John Player League and the commitment of counties to it meant that our Sunday afternoon matches in England had to be discontinued. However, there were a few tours and one-off matches of which the trip to Jamaica was one. We had one first-class match, against Jamaica at Sabina Park in Kingston, and a couple of minor matches, one against Central Jamaica and one against Jamaica Young Cricketers. It was all very relaxed – it is difficult not to relax in the land of Bob Marley, a beautiful and friendly island (away from the drugs and violence of downtown Kingston). Montego Bay was a lovely spot with great beaches and expensive properties, a playground for successful American businessmen who, to my astonishment, were pretty clued up on cricket.

It was a great opportunity to meet old friends and make some new ones. Ted Dexter was the captain. I learned a lot from him, both in terms of the technique of batting on hard wickets and approach to the game. Garry Sobers also joined us, one of the best all-rounders of all time and, despite his great ability, a very modest man with no airs and graces. Godfrey Evans accompanied us throughout the tour. It was educational to be able to learn from them both and to hear Godfrey reminisce on the return flight about the great players of his time like Len Hutton, Alec Bedser and Jim Laker.

I returned briefly to Pakistan in February 1971 to play a series of three first-class matches for an International XI against a BCCP XI in Karachi, Dacca and Lahore. Saeed played in the opposition on each occasion. The BCCP XI won one of the matches, the other two being left drawn. After that I played no more cricket in Pakistan for more than fifteen years.

I was to have a life ban imposed on me so there was no way I could have played there anyway but, as I have said, there is no way cricket and politics can be separated in Pakistan. From Partition onwards, politics have been volatile. I had no great desire to be in a country torn apart by violence, military coups, civil wars, assassinations, sabotage and death sentences on deposed political leaders. I was more than happy to see England as my home in summer with the opportunity to play cricket and work abroad in South Africa, Rhodesia and Australia during the northern hemisphere winter.

Gloria and I on our wedding day with my father,
Inyatullah Ahmed, and my mother, Shamim Akhtar.

5

Back to Surrey

I returned to The Oval a wounded soldier, feeling very disconsolate, uncertain of my future and at a crossroads. I sought a meeting with my captain, Micky Stewart. As always, he was prepared to give me his time.

I said that because of one man I saw no future for me in Pakistan cricket. I had lived five years in England, was fully adjusted to western culture and used to the playing conditions. Was there any way I might qualify to play for England? Having played for Pakistan very recently, I realised it might be a long time before I was entitled to do so. That was a decision for the Test and County Cricket Board. Micky suggested I write to Lord's, which I did. I received a sympathetic reply stating that as I had been in England for five years, if I had not already played for Pakistan I would have been eligible for consideration for the next England tour (to Australia in 1970/71). However, as I had already played Test cricket for another country, if I expressed a desire to play for England there would be a qualifying period of five years, during which I could not play for Pakistan again.

I seemed to have fallen between two stools. I was effectively excluded from Pakistan because of the high-handed intransigence of one man. But I was excluded from England too, firstly because of the strength of feeling in my family, and secondly because of the understandable qualification conditions designed (quite rightly) to prevent players from flipping between international teams at will. Five years and the 1976 season seemed a long way off (almost a quarter of a lifetime when you're twenty-two) but I thought I could make it. By that time Saeed would probably have retired from international cricket and the situation might be different. However, the TCCB subsequently changed the rules and the qualification period became seven years rather than five. That made the possibility of my playing for England more remote. Indeed, it was a bridge too far and never to happen.

My father, who was living in Wimbledon and working with the Pakistan Diplomatic Service in Knightsbridge, was extremely hurt at the way I had been treated by Kardar. However, it was my decision to try and qualify for England. My father reluctantly accepted that, in the circumstances, I had little alternative. The issue went on the back burner for a while and I got on with my cricket.

Commenting on a disappointing season in 1970, the Surrey Yearbook, while commending the entertainment value of the players (at least, some of them) mentioned the attendances, now – apart from one-day cricket – in decline after the post-war euphoria which had spilt over into the 1950s, aided and abetted in Surrey's case by a very successful team: 'Neither members nor the public are present in sufficient numbers to provide the background of support that a successful team needs ... Too few people in the last few seasons have savoured the joy of Younis in full flight, John Edrich's powerful solidity, Intikhab Alam's artistry and the explosive force, at his best, of Geoff Arnold.'

The 1971 edition of *Wisden*, however, was particularly critical of the team and of the captain: 'Another reason for disappointment [in addition to slow pitches] has been the leadership. Stewart has failed to get the best out of his gifted players, and his tactics have been unenterprising ... Moreover, they seemed to think too much about denying opponents rather than achieving something positive themselves.'

I could not disagree more. Micky Stewart had been captain for eight seasons and while I did not experience the early ones, I can honestly say that he was one of the most enterprising and knowledgeable captains I played under. In direct line of succession from Stuart Surridge, like all good captains, he was prepared to risk losing a match in order to win it and never afraid of giving the opposition a decent chance to win the game.

In those days, captains tended to be very defensive. It was three-day cricket and, particularly where rain had intervened on one or both of the first two, it was often down to a declaration on the final day. Some were quite unrealistic. As a general rule captains would rather draw games than risk losing them. In 1970, more than half the matches in the Championship ended in draws and other seasons in the late sixties and early seventies were very similar. It is perhaps no coincidence that it was around this time that the post-war boom in attendances at county matches began to decline as the public turned its support to one-day cricket where, assuming the weather didn't ruin a match, a result could be guaranteed and they could see both sides' leading batsmen and bowlers on the same day.

Settling for a draw was never Micky's way. He would go all out to make a match interesting, setting us specific targets: 'I need 278 by five past twelve'. 271 would not be good enough. If we needed to throw away wickets to achieve the target, then so be it. We were playing for Surrey, not for ourselves, as the dressing room was reminded when against Kent at Blackheath in 1969. He declared when I was on 98, taking the quite correct view that a Younis century was less significant than a Surrey victory. He had no time for boring draws, unlike many county captains who adopted a defensive approach and were quite happy to settle for avoiding defeat rather than dangling a carrot to encourage the opposition to go for a target, especially against the stronger counties; Yorkshire, Surrey and Kent.

There were a number of good spinners in the county game: David Acfield, Ray East and Robin Hobbs at Essex, David Allen and John Mortimore at Gloucestershire, Fred Titmus and Phil Edmonds at Middlesex, Jack Simmonds at Lancashire, Geoff Miller at Derbyshire and Derek Underwood at Kent. All were capable of bowling out a side on third-day pitches which were uncovered at this time, so it is perhaps surprising and disappointing that so many matches failed to reach a definite conclusion.

I had begun the 1970 season well against Northamptonshire with a steady 75 in the first innings, then 112 not out at breakneck speed. It enabled us to set up a declaration which challenged Northamptonshire to score 254 in just over three hours. Thanks to Hylton Ackerman's century, they did with three wickets to spare. It was a classic case of risking losing a match in order to win it and was an outstanding example of Micky's enterprising captaincy. There was a gap between *Wisden's* rhetoric and Stewart's reality. Again, in the following match at Hove, a third innings declaration set Sussex 276 to win in three and three-quarter hours. Having lost three wickets with the total on 21, they settled for a draw, but Surrey had made all the running. The Yorkshire match was rain-affected and there was no chance of a result, but John Edrich's two centuries at New Road again enabled Micky to set a fourth innings target of 219 in thirty-eight overs. They fell six short with two wickets left. Unenterprising tactics? Thinking more about avoiding defeat than winning?

My 66 not out contributed towards a declaration at Bournemouth and a ten-run win – but we could have lost. There were several similar instances. I hope I have said enough to disprove *Wisden's* summing up of the captain's tactics. My highest score that season was 120 not out against Somerset at The Oval with two sixes and seventeen fours in just over three hours.

The dressing room atmosphere at The Oval in those days was positive and vibrant and that was very much because of Micky's influence. He was always willing to discuss the technicalities of line, length and field placings and tactics with the senior players, though not at the expense of the younger players with whom he was equally generous with his time. However, his years at the helm were not good years for Surrey. Members and supporters hoped for a continuation of the golden age of the 1950s, but it was not to be. Other counties were growing stronger and Test calls didn't help. Bereft of players like Ken Barrington, Graham Roope and Geoff Arnold, the side was never going to be as strong and the county didn't help itself by recruiting players who were not good enough to be playing first-class cricket. The system was a bit hit and miss. Clubs would ring up and say 'So-and-so is looking good in weekend cricket. Will you give him a trial at The Oval?' The response was usually positive and a number of players were offered contracts who were not really good enough to proceed beyond the 2nd XI. During my qualifying period in 1965 and 1966 I had played a lot of second team cricket and I could see they were not up to it. I don't know why those who made the decisions were unable to see this. Furthermore, at Surrey and elsewhere, players used to arrive from the Universities (only Oxford and Cambridge had first-class status in those days) having played a handful of matches against the counties and thinking they were good enough to play first-class cricket. With rare exceptions they weren't.

In the John Player League, Surrey finished about halfway. My own limited overs performance that year, including the Gillette Cup, was much improved – five fifties and an average of 34. We had some exciting finishes, enhancing the value of the competition as entertainment, such as a win with two balls to spare against Northamptonshire. Tactically, too, we were becoming more astute, employing negative leg side bowling to secure a narrow win against Somerset. They were not very exciting tactics and soon to come under the scrutiny of those responsible for the regulations and playing conditions when such deliveries would receive harsher treatment from the umpires and be called wide.

Lancashire won the league for the second consecutive season, gaining themselves a trophy and £1,000. There were various bits and pieces of additional sponsorship, like a pot of £1,000 being available for the number of sixes hit. 434 of them meant each one was worth £2 6s 1d (just over £2.30 in the decimal currency introduced the following year) – insignificant compared with the riches now on offer in the IPL, but welcome enough at the time.

Two of my half centuries came in the Gillette Cup where we had a good run, beating Yorkshire at Harrogate where snow stopped play for ten minutes, then Glamorgan on a tricky pitch at Swansea, an outstanding eight-run win against Middlesex, before finally coming unstuck against Sussex in a tight finish at The Oval. Lancashire added to their John Player League triumph by winning another one-day trophy for their cabinet.

The following season, Micky Stewart answered his critics in the best possible way – not by engaging in debate through the media, but on the field letting bat and ball do the talking – leading the county to their first Championship title since 1958. It was an isolated victory, the last one before the triumph of Adam Hollioake's team in 1999.

The odds seemed stacked against winning the Championship. Edrich was on Test duty for much of the summer, Mike Edwards lost form and was then injured and, as the Yearbook pointed out, there was often pressure on the middle order – Graham Roope, Stewart Storey and myself – to rescue an indifferent start, build an innings and keep an eye on the bonus points, one point for every 25 runs over 150 in the first eighty-five overs of the first innings.

It was very close indeed in the end. Having been in the top four for most of the season, we suddenly fell away almost to mid-table, bouncing back at the end to finish with the same number of points as Warwickshire. We took the title on the tie-breaker of most wins. Warwickshire had more bonus points, introduced to encourage more positive cricket, but in the end, whatever peripheral points systems are introduced, the game is about winning, so it was absolutely fair that Surrey's eleven wins should shade Warwickshire's nine. We went into our last match at Southampton needing six points to be assured of first place. We managed only four batting points on the Saturday, but on the Monday morning scraped the additional two. We went on to lose the match, which wasn't part of the script, but John Edrich's fine batting was matched by that of Barry Richards and Roy Marshall. Nevertheless, we celebrated with champagne on the pitch. It was the first title since the glory days of the fifties – beyond the memory of some of the younger members of the team.

I recently met Pat Pocock after many years – he is now President of Surrey County Cricket Club – and we were able to reminisce pleasantly, as older players do, about shared experiences and matches of forty and more years ago. Pat was a good, honest team man for whom I have always had the greatest respect. He remembered in particular the Championship winning season of 1971 and the important innings I played as a contribution to it.

My own season was not the best, but I still managed to finish third in the averages behind John Edrich and Graham Roope, with 1,326 runs at 37.88, with just the one century, 138 not out against Leicestershire at Grace Road, during which I shared a fourth wicket partnership of 226 with Roope.

It has been suggested that my arrogance antagonised other teammates, in particular John Edrich and Graham Roope. I have no recollection of this. After all, we all toured South Africa reasonably amicably as colleagues. Certainly I was to have my differences with John later, but not at this stage; and I never had any problems with Graham. We batted together on many occasions and much later, when our playing careers were over, we did some work together for Eagle Star and advertised the services of the company in *The Cricketer* in 1989.

Once again we finished mid-table in the John Player League, but had a run to the quarter-finals of the Gillette Cup with a straightforward win over Hertfordshire (in the competition because of their placing in the Minor Counties Championship the previous season), then a narrower one against Middlesex before bowing out to Gloucestershire, failing to score twenty to win from the final five overs with three wickets in hand.

Pakistan toured England that year, sharing a twin-tour with India. They lost one Test and drew the other two, and would surely have won at Edgbaston had not rain washed out most of the final day. A great find was Zaheer Abbas, recalled to the team after being dropped following our shared debut, who had a double century in the Edgbaston Test. Zaheer passed 1,500 first-class runs before the tour ended in mid-July with a match against Surrey at The Oval, where Intikhab spun his country to an eight-wicket victory over his own county side. Saeed was vice-captain on the tour and it was disappointing that he did not feature in the Surrey match. Included in the Pakistan team, however, was an eighteen-year-old hopeful by the name of Imran Khan. He batted towards the end of the order and bowled a bit, but did not impress as being anything out of the ordinary. His roots were in Lahore, though I did not recall ever coming across him there. He was five years my junior and from a different social background, so it is unlikely that our paths crossed at school, on the cricket field or socially.

Raw and inexperienced at this stage of his career, I recall being told by John Jameson, Warwickshire and England opening batsman and later a first-class umpire and Assistant Secretary of MCC, that on one occasion, Imran's accuracy – or lack of It – was such that he began an innings with an over of thirteen deliveries from most of which the square leg umpire was in more danger than the batsman.

However, Imran worked incredibly hard at his game and went on to captain Oxford University, play for Worcestershire and Sussex, captain his country, win a World Cup and challenge Garry Sobers as the world's leading all-rounder. I could never count Imran as a friend, but am full of admiration for the way he developed his talents and his career.

Despite the Championship win, not all was sweetness and light in Kennington. A young fast bowler by the name of Bob Willis, who had been called into the MCC side touring Australia the previous winter and met with some success there, could not command a regular place in the side because of the presence of Arnold and Jackman. He was not awarded a county cap, generally thought to be more than deserved, and took himself off to play for Warwickshire.

Micky Stewart had indicated that he wished to relinquish the captaincy at the end of the season, but was asked by the committee to stay on. He eventually agreed but asked for faster pitches with more bounce and carry at The Oval and wished to see more games played out in the county, away from headquarters, because of the poor attendances and what he saw as a lack of atmosphere.

Surrey finished twelfth in the 1972 Championship table, now reduced to twenty matches to make way for another limited overs competition. The Benson and Hedges was a one-day competition based on four regional groups then a knockout, played over 55 overs per side, but there were reserve days. Three of our four zonal matches went to a second day and one to a third. We failed to qualify for the quarter-finals, having won two and lost two and failed to get a bonus point for bowling out the opposition.

The competition was originally sponsored for two years with a total of £80,000 on offer, compared with John Players' £12,000ish per annum. Sponsorship was taking off and the original two years became thirty until the competition was eclipsed by the juggernaut of Twenty20.

There was no doubt, Surrey's season was poor. There were now four trophies to play for and Surrey came no-where near winning any of them. 'Riches to rags – and hard to bear,' said Arthur McIntyre. Micky gave up the captaincy, a year after he first indicated he wanted to, after ten seasons in the job. He was succeeded by John Edrich, who did it for five years before handing it on to Roger Knight. My own season, said *Wisden*, was inconsistent, 'although he played some brilliant innings'.

I cannot leave 1972, however, without mentioning an extraordinary spell of bowling by Pat Pocock against Sussex at Eastbourne which almost won us a match which looked destined to be lost. *Wisden* records: 'The Surrey off-spinner took seven wickets for four runs in his last two overs, leaving Sussex three runs short of their target with one wicket left. The scorebook recorded his, and the game's final over as WWW1W1, with a second run attempted off the last ball leading to the dismissal of Doshi.' It was the only time in first-class cricket that five wickets had fallen in the same over.

At the end of the 1972 season, Gloria and I were married, first fulfilling the legal requirements at Merton Register Office, then adjourning to the Dog and Fox in Wimbledon for an Islamic ceremony. It was a happy day, though there were inevitably tensions as it was impossible to ignore the cultural differences. Gloria was a non-prac-tising Roman Catholic but agreed to wear Islamic dress for the occasion. My father had serious reservations, not because he thought east was east and west was west and never the twain should meet, but he thought that I was too young to be married. I was coming up to twenty-five, but he took the view that I should be concentrating on my cricket career rather than taking on the additional responsibility of a wife and potential family. With the benefit of hindsight, he was 100% correct.

There was, however, no personal animosity towards Gloria. Quite the contrary, in fact. She was welcomed into the family and had spent time with them when I was away in Pakistan. Keen to learn about Muslim faith and traditions, she later converted to Islam and has been to Mecca and performed the Hajj seven times.

Enjoy
Coca-Cola
TRADE MARK REGD

Younis Ahmed

Padding up for South Australia,
supported by my sponsor, Coca Cola.

6

In Giants' Footsteps

I was stunned. Sir Donald Bradman had been following my progress in English cricket, reading reports and questioning people, finding out what kind of person I was off the field. He wrote to Geoffrey Howard, the Surrey County Cricket Club Secretary at the time, and was a big influence in encouraging me to follow in the distinguished steps of Sir Garfield Sobers and Barry Richards and become the overseas player for South Australia in the 1972/73 season. I could scarcely believe it.

There was no way I could begin to compare myself with Barry, who was without a doubt one of the best batsmen ever to have played the game. I played against him when he starred for Hampshire and was to do so again when he opened for South Africa against the Derrick Robins XI. He had so much grace and so much time to play the ball and was so elegant and confident playing against the quicks. That is not to say that he could not play spin bowling too. His bat looked to be about twice the width of the three stumps. I admired the way he could take an attack apart and play every stroke in the book. He could certainly turn it on when he wanted to get a big hundred and perhaps the only flaw in his game was that he seemed to find batting so easy that he would get bored and get himself out.

Against Western Australia he scored an almost unbelievable 325 in a day, 356 overall in 381 balls against an attack which included Dennis Lillee, Graham McKenzie and Tony Lock – not the worst in the world. After only one season in the Sheffield Shield, however, he decided to return to South Africa. Before him, the overseas player at Adelaide was Garry Sobers. It was also a great pleasure to see Sobers play the game. Give him a bat, any bat: give him a ball and with either pace or spin, he could walk into the strongest side in the world, bowling whatever style at any time and batting in any position. I remember sitting in the plane on the way to Australia thinking, 'How do I follow those two?'

Barry had a very successful season both with South Australia and with Prospect, the club for which I was to play. At the time there were just eight inter-state matches and when there was no state fixture you were expected to play for your club, practising in the week, one evening with the state side and one with the club.

My appointment had no effect on the South Australia budget, my salary and expenses being met by Coca Cola. In addition, I was paid a dollar a run. Greg Chappell and Terry Jenner were also sponsored by Coca Cola and, as well as playing state and grade cricket, we were required to conduct coaching sessions in colleges, schools and at the university. It was great fun. I certainly learned a lot about coaching from two great blokes.

Grade cricket in Australia (and the parallel system in South Africa) is particularly strong. While the swing to limited overs cricket is now recognised, including Twenty20 competitions, the main grade competitions are played over two days, making the transition from grade to first-class cricket a smoother one than in England where a limited amount of two-day club cricket has been tried and abandoned. Furthermore, Australian club players have the opportunity to test themselves against state and international cricketers and try to impress the selectors. In short, the transition from club to state to international cricket is a smoother one and there is less likelihood of talent being overlooked.

I didn't know at the time, but my signing for South Australia was strongly opposed by the temperamental state and country captain, Ian Chappell. I'm not aware that he had any other overseas player in mind. He simply took the view that there was no need for an overseas player and local talent should be encouraged. He did all the right things when I arrived, welcoming me and introducing me to all the other players, but he also made no attempt to hide his displeasure and gradually distanced himself from me as the season progressed.

There was a bit of a power struggle in South Australian cricket and I was caught in the middle. As a successful captain of both state and country, Chappell (Chappelli, as he was widely known, because that's how his name appeared on the scoreboard) thought he did not have sufficient power. Conversely, Bradman thought he had too much and felt obliged to apologise to me for Chappell's attitude.

Whatever Chappell's view of my signing might have been, once we were on the field together there was absolutely no animosity. Yes, he was a tough captain and a tough character, but on the occasions we batted together, he was nothing but utterly supportive and helpful, telling me when I arrived at the crease who was swinging it, who was turning it, how much and which way.

I did have the dubious privilege of witnessing Ian Chappell's fiery temper. Opposition captains and bowlers knew that he found it difficult to resist the hook and bounced him to tempt him into playing it. On one such occasion, falling into the trap, he was caught in the deep off the top edge for not very many and the dressing room suffered on his return.

He came back into the changing area and smashed his bat against the lockers. There was a table in the middle of the room on which was orange juice, cold water, glasses and so on. He smashed a glass on the table which inevitably broke, sending broken glass everywhere, including into Chappell's hand. He needed quite a few stitches. His brother Greg was quite the opposite. One of the most elegant batsmen it has been my pleasure to play with or against, he was always a gentleman.

During my time in Australia, I had the opportunity to face both Dennis Lillee and Jeff Thompson, scourges of England and other international teams later in the decade. Thompson was the quickest I ever faced. Those of an earlier generation would say Frank Tyson, but Thompson was doubly difficult in that he brought his arm from behind his back in a slingy sort of action, giving you a split-second to see the ball and react. With most bowlers it's possible to watch the ball in the hand and get an idea in advance whether it's going to move and which way. Not so with Jeff. It was on you before you realised. By contrast, Lillee was the more intelligent bowler. He would watch you at the crease, test you with a few just outside off stump down the corridor of uncertainty, see how you reacted to that and bowl accordingly. He was never easy to face and always kept you guessing. He was a bowler with a big heart.

It was on Australia's faster, bouncier pitches that I learned to play with confidence off the back foot. Pakistan had been across the line; England straight and on the front foot to counteract the seam or spin. Now I added the cut and pull to my repertoire, an advantage at the Adelaide Oval where there was more reward playing to the short, square boundaries rather than the long straight ones.

I recall a match at the MCG, Victoria v South Australia, attended by perhaps 10,000 spectators. It would have filled most English county grounds, but they were almost imperceptible in that vast coliseum. About ten times that crowd would attend the Grand Final of the VFL (Victorian Football League – AFL now). I was twelfth man, although as one or two of the team felt a bit hot and decided to have a rest in the pavilion, I was on the field most of the time. Keith Stackpole, Paul Sheahan and Ian Redpath piled up over 400 runs, declaring with three wickets down. The playing area was vast and I did a lot of leather chasing in the course of that innings.

I enjoyed my time with South Australia, although it took me a while to adjust to the pace of Australian pitches. Expectations among the Australian public were high, although I had only a modest season; for the state too it was a disappointing one. For much of the time it looked as though we were to take the Sheffield Shield, but a late surge by Western Australia who won their last three matches outright ensured that they retained the title.

I was, of course, overawed to meet Sir Donald Bradman and found him a very modest man. Those who have reached the top of their tree usually are. Humble and self-effacing, he did not speak about his own very considerable achievements in the game unless asked to do so. When asked about the bodyline tour of 1932/33, there was no bitterness or rancour. He limited himself to saying that Jardine had a plan and, as England won the series, it obviously worked for him. He had nothing malicious to say about Jardine or his tactics. That, I thought, was very gracious of him. It was unbelievable to talk to him, this great man who worked out that most wickets fell to catches and consequently hardly ever hit a ball in the air. The art of batting was to keep the ball on the ground. I was flattered that he was much more interested in what we were doing than in what he had done.

The lifestyle in Adelaide was congenial and Gloria and I were made very welcome. Gloria was a Sydney girl who did not know Adelaide; we both loved the outdoors and thoroughly enjoyed ourselves, finding a South Australian summer much preferable to an English winter. We made many great friends, in cricket circles and outside, who made us welcome in their homes and gave us a taste of the world-famous Australian hospitality. There were some fantastic parties and Glenelg beach was only a short tram ride away. There was still time to get there after practice, have a swim and watch the sunset.

Meanwhile, Pakistan were touring in the same country in which I was playing. A week after signing my contract and three years after I played my two Tests against New Zealand, I received a letter inviting me to join the Pakistan camp for the tour of Australia and New Zealand. I wrote back, declining the offer on the grounds that I wished to qualify for England and because I had already signed a contract with South Australia. It would have added an extra complication. Maybe I was cutting off my nose to spite my face, but having made a commitment to the TCCB and to South Australia, I felt it would be dishonourable to renege on those.

I realised that I had now burnt my boats and sacrificed any hope of playing again for Pakistan. It was a conclusion confirmed by the Pakistan Cricket Board twelve months later when my decision to tour South Africa resulted in a lifetime ban. It might not have made any difference anyway. Pakistan lost a hastily cobbled together Test series 3-0, the three matches played back to back around Christmas and New Year with no recovery time in between – pretty much par for the course now, but unusual at the time. They did rather better in New Zealand, winning one Test and drawing the other two.

It would have been good to play for the state side against them, but the tight schedule allowed no time for such a fixture, although there were matches against the other states. As is inevitably the case with Pakistani teams, controversy was never far away. The Test series defeat was met with the usual response of changing the captain. Intikhab Alam was replaced by Majid Khan.

The autocratic despotism of Abdul Hafeez Kardar was again in evidence. It has been said that Pakistanis are good cricketers and nice people, but poor organisers. With Kardar, only one of those is correct. He was certainly a very good cricketer and captain who worked hard at his game. He was also an outstanding organiser, almost single-handedly putting Pakistan cricket on the map in its early years. But not many people liked him. He was a man with no personal sensitivity and apparently no conscience about wrecking the lives and careers of those who crossed him.

Three years previously he had stripped Saeed of the captaincy, finished Hanif's career and delayed the blossoming of Zaheer's and my own. Now Kardar finished the Test careers of my brother Saeed and my former school friend, captain and club colleague, Mohammad Ilyas. Saeed claimed he had an injured back and was not available for the third Test in Sydney, but he was not believed. Words had been exchanged on the field with Dennis Lillee during the second Test in Melbourne. Lillee was pawing the ground and breathing revenge and there were hints that Saeed pulled out because he did not wish to face him. Not many would from choice, but few people know Saeed as I do – he would not pull out of a match for that reason. Fazal Mahmood has described Saeed as 'the bravest batsman Pakistan ever had'. Certainly Saeed respected Lillee as a bowler and, had he been fit, would have relished the challenge. If he said he was unfit, then he was unfit.

Osman Samiuddin refers to a finger rather than a back injury and says Saeed refused to play because, according to Zafar Altaf, Assistant Manager on the tour, the pitch was too green. Unlikely. Samiuddin also cites a hotel manager as saying that Saeed wrote a telegram in his own blood to President General Bhutto, complaining about the management. Why? Telegrams by definition are transmitted telegraphically. There would be no sign of blood by the time it reached the presidential office.

Nevertheless, Saeed was withdrawn from the New Zealand leg of the tour, his hotel bills allegedly unpaid by the management, and sent back to Pakistan where he received one of Kardar's liberally distributed life bans after playing one more match before the end of the season. His last first-class match was more than four years later when, his ban lifted, he was hauled out of retirement to play for the North West Province Frontier Governor's XI against the touring England side. After that, Saeed dabbled a bit in politics, supporting Mustafa Khan, governor of the Punjab. He then involved himself with Tableeghi Jamaat, the mass religious movement, has become a preacher, wears the traditional shalwar kameez and lives a devout life.

The demise of Mohammad Ilyas was even more colourful and dramatic. The *Who's Who of Cricketers* says blandly that his Test career ended on a controversial note during the 1972/73 tour to Australia and that he remained in Australia after the season ended. He was always a volatile character and there were disciplinary issues. During a discussion on one of these he aimed a blow at Kardar – hardly the best means of making a case for the defence. The result was that he was abandoned by the management, his hotel bill unpaid, spent a night on a park bench and subsequently played grade cricket for Waverley in Sydney.

Peter Oborne has a scarcely credible story, based on an interview with Ilyas, that his wallet, luggage and passport were confiscated and that he was obliged to spend not one but 'several' nights on the park bench before being recognised and rescued by Gamini Goonesena, formerly of Ceylon and Nottinghamshire, who arranged for him to apply for Australian citizenship and obtain an Australian passport. He married an Australian girl and came to England, but did not return to Pakistan until General Zia's military coup brought down the Bhutto government. Later, he became a selector and eventually Chairman of Selectors. Mohammad was proof that there was life after Pakistan cricket – proof that would have been of comfort to me, since I was about to receive a lifetime ban.

Embracing non-white cricket in Soweto.

7

Challenging Apartheid

Towards the end of the 1973 season I received a phone call at The Oval from millionaire businessman Derrick Robins, who enquired whether I might be available for an overseas tour. Having nothing in particular planned for that winter, I said I would like to know more about it. He was coming to the ground to watch the cricket that day. Could we meet afterwards for a chat and a meal? I readily agreed and it was only when we met that he revealed that the tour was to be to South Africa.

It would be a political hot potato. South Africa was banned from international cricket at the time because of its apartheid policy of racial discrimination. Robins felt something ought to be done. He was no supporter of the Nationalist Government or its policies, but thought that if he used some of his fortune to promote a multi-racial tour to the republic, he might encourage progress to a more equal society and better opportunities for the blacks, Indians and coloureds through sport. He intended funding the whole thing himself. There was no funding from the South African Government or any sporting organisation in South Africa.

Derrick Robins' name was not unknown. He was a self-made successful businessman who began with a cement mixer in a field before turning his Banbury Buildings into a major public company. He was also Chairman of Coventry City Football Club and, with Jimmy Hill as manager, took them from relative obscurity to a place in Division One (later the Premier League) where they remained for thirty-four seasons.

Robins had organised matches in England against the Universities and the Services. I had played in a few of those including one at Eastbourne under the captaincy of Richie Benaud. Furthermore, at the instigation of Jack Cheetham, former captain of South Africa and now a leading administrator, a Derrick Robins XI had toured South Africa in 1972/73; but that was an all-white, all-English, team. Neither the previous year's tour nor the planned one were considered rebel tours in the way those of the eighties were, but by that time political feeling was stronger and demonstrations better orchestrated and organised.

There were debates in the British media as to whether sport and politics could be kept separate and opinion was polarised. The result of a 4,000-member vote at a MCC special meeting was that they believed that the continuation of sporting links was the best way forward. Others, like Rev David Sheppard, Mike Brearley and John Arlott, believed that sporting links should be severed and that normal sport was impossible in an abnormal society. In between there were various shades of opinion and many were unable to make up their minds.

There was no such equivocation in Pakistan. From the time of its foundation, politics and cricket had been inextricably linked. Mohammad Ali Jinnah, the nation's founder, was proposed as the first Chairman of the Pakistan Cricket Board (in the event, illness and death prevented his taking up the role) and the national cricket team was seen as a source of national pride and an icon for Pakistan nationalism. To a largely non-white nation, the theory and practice of apartheid were abhorrent, so consequently, there were no links in any sport at any level, no trade and the passport was not valid for entry to the Republic of South Africa.

If further evidence is needed of the inseparability of politics and cricket in Pakistan, it can be found in the fact that many managers on the country's overseas tours have been government ministers or military men, charming and polished in the public relations aspects of the job, sound managers of men with strong organisational skills (much needed, given the propensity of the nation, especially its cricketers, to chaos and disorganisation), but with negligible knowledge of cricket and ignorant of the difference between a googly and a bouncer.

I reminded Derrick that India and Pakistan had no diplomatic relations with South Africa and prohibition on visiting South Africa was written in their passports. By this time I was the holder of both Pakistan and British passports, so I could get round it, but I knew it would be a hugely unpopular and much criticised move, especially in my native land where I still had roots. I needed to speak to my friends, family and captain before taking such a huge step.

Most people with whom I discussed the situation were either against me going or undecided. My father, mother, three brothers and a sister were at this time all living in Wimbledon, so I was not short of advice. It was, however, conflicting. Saeed, I knew, would be totally opposed. I reasoned, however, that the Pakistani people, including Saeed, had no direct experience of the country. I should give greater weight to the opinions of those who lived there or those from the UK and Australia whose passports did not restrict them from visiting South Africa. All recognised it was a difficult decision. Was I to criticise South African politics from afar or was I to go out there and try and make a difference, however forlorn that hope might be?

After several sleepless nights, I came down in favour of the latter. Why did I go? It was not the money, attractive though that was. £100 per week over eight weeks (all players were on the same pay), probably worth about ten times that now, was not to be sniffed at. Expenses and a bit of sunshine on top and cutting out the necessity of finding a winter job was an attractive proposition for a professional cricketer at a time when the typical pay of a capped player was just over £2,000.

For me though, the real reason was quite different. In simple terms, what the South African Government was doing – denying human rights to a huge majority of its citizens – was wrong. It would also be wrong if I turned my back on an opportunity to do something about it.

Two wrongs don't make a right. It was an opportunity that might not present itself again. Ultimately the decision was mine.

The tour was multi-racial only to the extent that an otherwise all-white team would include myself and John Shepherd of Barbados and Kent. The criticism that we were the token non-whites was inevitable, but to get round the stringent colour bar laws we were accorded the bizarre status of 'honorary whites'. While there would be no problems in the hotels where we would be treated as 'normal' white guests, in downtown restaurants and places designated as 'white' under the Group Areas Act we were allocated a minder to ensure our safety and civil treatment.

What some saw as a gesture, others, including *Wisden*, saw as being of historical significance: 'Another page of cricket history was written when the South African Government sanctioned the inclusion of Younis Ahmed of Pakistan, and the West Indian John Shepherd and these two great sportsmen were acclaimed and accepted wherever they went.'

The tour received much press publicity in the republic, the *Rand Daily Mail* emphasising the 'international' aspects, albeit slightly exaggerated as the only non-English players, apart from John and myself, were Bruce Francis and Johnny Gleeson from Australia. There was some interest in the fancy wide-lapelled white-and-gold braided blazers, and some attention on those who had toured in the previous season and had come again, but most curiosity focused on the motivation of the two honorary whites.

When asked how he had responded to those who had advised him not to come, Shepherd expressed surprise and replied nobody had asked him not to come. It almost certainly wasn't true, there being no stronger opponents of apartheid than the West Indies Cricket Board. I said something similar. That wasn't true either, but it seemed the right thing to say. In response to criticism that Shepherd was perpetuating apartheid, he answered, 'My only purpose in coming here is to play cricket, and if you don't mind, we'll leave it at that.' I stuck to the same line: 'It's going to be a great tour, and I'm going to enjoy my cricket.' Meanwhile, our captain Brian Close sidestepped political issues, saying simply that his team had come to play winning cricket.

Our first match was to be in Soweto. This was the sharp end of apartheid – a massive shanty town where over a million blacks, who by law had to be back there by dusk every evening, struggled in appalling conditions to eke out a subsistence level existence. The captain, Sam Nteshikisa, recalled playing with white boys but only before the war and the advent of the Nationalist Government in 1948, after which much of what was custom and practice in the way of segregation became enshrined in law. He welcomed the change in attitude, small though it was, over the last ten years.

It was the first occasion that an overseas touring team had played an official fixture against an African XI. The Africans were outclassed – by Surrey as it happened, Graham Roope and John Edrich scoring centuries. I chipped in later with 37. They were totally unable to read John Gleeson who cleaned up with seven for 33. John Shepherd, my co-honorary white, performed superbly both on and off the field, hitting some of the biggest sixes ever seen anywhere. We broke the ice. He was the star of the show, but the result did not matter. A breakthrough had been made.

We were happy to give away some of our cricket gear to a dedicated and enthusiastic but poverty-stricken team who were nevertheless desperate to join the cricket scene and play on the international stage. It was a view shared by the white South African cricketers we played against. The obstacle was not the players but the government. That had to change – and would.

The evening before the match, news came through that I had received a lifetime ban from the Pakistan Cricket Board because of my decision to tour South Africa. I was not naive enough to assume that my presence on the tour would be disregarded by the authorities in Pakistan. Nevertheless it was disappointing that the ban came without my ever being given the opportunity to explain my position or my reasons for visiting the country. In democratic countries, except where a state of emergency exists, even those on criminal charges are given an opportunity to defend themselves and state their case. Innocent until proved guilty is the general understanding. My treatment was the opposite of that. I was grateful for the support from Derrick Robins, manager Les Ames, captain Brian Close and several other members of the team in seeing me through a very difficult time.

I remain firmly convinced that the decision to ban me was taken by Abdul Hafeez Kardar acting alone. He had his own scores to settle. Twelve months earlier I had declined an invitation to join the Pakistan party to tour Australia because I was already committed to my contract with South Australia. Furthermore, when Chairman of the Pakistan Selection Committee he had had his differences with Saeed. When I had played in my two Test matches in 1969 he had not been impressed when I expressed my dissatisfaction at being omitted from the team for the final Test in Dacca – I thought I was at least entitled to travel and be part of the squad.

I knew that as long as Kardar stayed there would always be a serious problem and I would never be given a chance. I have never had a problem with the people of Pakistan, nor with its cricketers, but I felt that one man was hampering my career and there was little or nothing I could do about it. For seventeen years, during much of which I was playing at my best, I was denied the opportunity of playing international cricket. And that was down to one man, the same man who finished Hanif's career and dropped Zaheer Abbas from the Test side after one match following eight first-class centuries. There were no checks and balances.

British relations with South Africa were far more relaxed than those of Pakistan. There was political activism against South Africa, but there was no trade boycott. Rugby continued to be played – though at times in difficult circumstances and stretching police and security resources to the full. Peter Hain and his supporters had organised themselves into STST (Stop the Seventy Tour) to bring disruption to the South Africa rugby tour to England that winter and had been generally successful in obstructing matches and hotel and travel arrangements, causing more than a little embarrassment to players, organisers and governments. Since the D'Oliveira affair no Test cricket had been played, although English professionals continued to coach and play in South Africa during the northern hemisphere close season. David Bairstow, Richard Lumb, Clive Radley, Ashley Harvey-Walker and Barry Stead all played for clubs in the Transvaal Premier League alongside club and provincial cricketers. Don Wilson was coaching in the townships. Graham Roope was playing in Kimberley.

I honestly believed that as a non-white sportsman in the country, I might help to change it for the better. Though apartheid was to remain in place for another sixteen years or so, the attitudes I encountered from people I met, including leading politicians, suggested that might not be as long as that. Although there were and still are hardline Afrikaners who firmly believed that apartheid was the correct and only sensible political system, there was a general feeling that change was inevitable and there should be cooperation between the Nationalist Government and the black African National Congress (ANC) to ensure a peaceful transition. Sport – especially cricket and rugby – could play a crucial part of that process.

It was good to get away from the politics and play a bit of cricket, though obviously politics was never very far away. Thankfully the tour was blessedly free from political demonstrations, which could have easily spilled over into violence.

After matches against Orange Free State, Griqualand West, Border and Northern Transvaal under Gillette Cup Rules and first-class ones against Western Province at Newlands and Natal at Kingsmead, we played Transvaal, over the years the most successful provincial side at the Wanderers in Johannesburg. The ground is popularly known as the Bull Ring, because of its circular shape and high tiered bench seating. Transvaal batted first and made 217. We replied the following day, a Saturday. The ground was full of South Africans of all races, deprived of international cricket, though the blacks and coloureds had their own areas. We lost two wickets for 112 and I was in on a pitch that rivalled the WACA in Perth as the hardest and fastest in the world. For the first two or three overs I struggled to get used to the bounce. My first aim was to survive for half an hour. It was important not to get out. I felt I was batting not for myself but for the millions of underprivileged blacks, coloured and Indians that made up the large radio audience (no television in South Africa in those days) and to prove a point to the Government officials in the main Long Room. I received a great reception for my fifty, but no way was I going to get out before reaching three figures. I went on to get a century. The reception was amazing.

Wisden records that, 'On the second day, Younis took the Wanderers by storm. The brilliant Pakistani reached a scintillating hundred in two hours, twenty-six minutes, and was given another standing ovation twenty minutes later as he returned to the pavilion after scoring 123. His West Indian colleague Shepherd, had the crowd on its feet as he pulverised the Transvaal attack for a hurricane 39 which included two sixes and six fours. He and Tolchard added 50 in nineteen minutes, the wicketkeeper's share being a single.'

The standing ovation for my innings lasted about two minutes. The whites in the stadium were happy for me because they knew in their hearts that Younis Ahmed and John Shepherd were sending a message to the Government: if you were to open up your all-white sports facilities you would produce many Basil D'Oliveiras, many John Shepherds and many Younis Ahmeds for the world. Accompanying the Government officials in the Long Room were leading South African cricketers of recent years, including Jack Cheetham, Jackie McGlew and Ali Bacher. I think they appreciated that John Shepherd and I had made ourselves vulnerable to criticism by playing in South Africa. Telegrams of congratulation came from my parents in London saying, 'Younis, we are proud of you.' Messages of congratulation and flowers were sent to my hotel. It would take time, but the barriers were beginning to crumble.

At a reception that evening I was approached by the Minister for Sport, Dr Piet Koornhof who said, 'Younis, thank you. You can never know what you have done for our country.' I don't think I have ever been happier. It was the beginning of a road which, forty-three years later, was to lead to Temba Bavuma, raised in the Cape Township of Langa, becoming the first black South African cricketer to score a Test century.

Koornhof had an interesting political career. There are exceptions, but over their lifetime, people's political sympathies tend to move from left to right. Students with no or very little money tend to be left-leaning, then as they earn an income and perhaps inherit assets, they appreciate they have something to conserve and move to the right. Koornhof's political journey was the opposite of that. Educated at the leading Afrikaans University of Stellenbosch and at Oxford where he was a Rhodes scholar, he joined the National Party, worked directly for Prime Minister Hendrik Verwoerd and was Secretary of the Broederbond, a white supremacist organisation, about as far to the right as it was possible to get, even in apartheid South Africa. Then, on joining the Government, he moved rapidly through a series of senior ministerial posts, including Sport, Energy and Immigration. However, on advising Prime Minister, PW Botha, that the prospect of bloodshed in the country would be reduced if Nelson Mandela were released from his Robben Island prison, he was sidelined from mainstream government and appointed Ambassador to the United States of America. On his return, he fathered five children with a coloured girl and later joined the ANC.

At the time I met him, racial integration was not in his mind and he was still advocating separate national sports teams for separate ethnic groups. Many people misunderstood my touring in South Africa. I had come as a cricketer, not a politician, but I have often wondered how far my century and our brief conversation that Saturday evening at the Wanderers went towards changing his mind. It is naive to believe that sport can be separated from politics and I hoped that in some small way I had contributed to black and coloured peoples being freed from the oppression of apartheid.

The tour ended with three matches against a South African Invitation XI, dubbed mini-Tests by the media, against something pretty close to what would have been the Test side had not South Africa been banned from international cricket at the time. We managed creditable draws in the first two, but came unstuck in the last one, losing at the Wanderers by an innings and 83 runs thanks to Eddie Barlow's double century and Lee Irvine's supporting 125. The fast pitch suited the Springboks' quicks, Mike Procter, Rupert Hanley and Vintcent van der Bijl. We didn't help ourselves by leaving out John Snow as a disciplinary measure.

A match scheduled for five days was finished in four and it was some small consolation to win the limited overs match, hastily arranged to fill the last day. There was to have been another match against an African XI in Port Elizabeth, but the match had unfortunately to be cancelled because of a waterlogged pitch.

From a playing point of view, it was a successful tour; from mine especially as I topped the batting averages with just over 50. John Edrich was close behind with 49, but he seemed uncomfortable in my presence and I detected a resentment and jealousy that was to continue in future years. More important than team or individual performances, however, was the impact we were able to make on our hosts, demonstrating that multi-racial sport was possible in a deeply divided South African society.

I became very friendly with Joe Pamensky, the President of the South African Cricket Union, a man highly respected by all the communities in South Africa and one who was always available for help and advice. I had the pleasure of meeting him when we arrived in Johannesburg. He worked tirelessly to open doors for non-white cricketers in South Africa. It was his belief that sport should be free from political interference and he had made several trips to England to meet TCCB and ICC officials at Lord's. We got on very well from the first time I met him. He was also very approachable, very knowledgeable about the game. I feel greatly honoured to call him my good friend.

After 1993, when I went back to South Africa and opened my own Cricket Academy in Johannesburg, although he was no longer President, Joe was a constant source of help and advice and established contacts for me to get the business off the ground. He encouraged me and was very pleased about my idea of an academy. I am still in touch with him. He has given and continues to give much of his time to cricket, watching every ball of every Test match whenever he can. He had a close relationship with Sir Donald Bradman and South African cricket was very fortunate to have him as one of its senior officials. I also had the pleasure of meeting and becoming acquainted with Wilfred Isaacs, who spent much of his time and money on tours within South Africa and overseas to England. I remember playing against his team for a Surrey XI in 1969. I scored a century in that match and was presented with his touring tie.

After the eight-week tour of South Africa in 1973/74, at the instigation of Judge Ahmed Ebrahim, I was offered a three-month contract to captain and coach Universals, a racially-mixed club in Salisbury, Rhodesia. Ebrahim, later an ICC Match Referee and perhaps more significantly appointed to Zimbabwe's Supreme Court, was deposed by the Mugabe Government. A critic of that regime, he was given the choice of resignation or imprisonment and took the former. I was invited back for 1974/75, one of three very enjoyable seasons. They looked after me well, providing me with a house and car. I was very lucky to have made so many wonderful friends, including the Moosa family, Kassim Abdullah, Bob Bardolia and several other families. My son Samir was born in Rhodesia in January 1975.

Rhodesia was a country about which I knew nothing at the time, but know a bit more now. Once known as the 'breadbasket of Africa' it has now, as Zimbabwe, according to some sections of the media, become more of an African basketcase. It has been sad to see the decline of a potentially affluent nation. After the Unilateral Declaration of Independence in 1965, Ian Smith's Government was dependent on South African finance, but as economic sanctions began to bite, that dried up. After a period of civil war, Robert Mugabe took over, first as Prime Minister, then as President. Since then, the country's economy has spiralled downwards, despite massive mineral wealth in the form of gold, diamonds and emeralds, plus tobacco. I saw the unrest that would lead to national disharmony, but never did I imagine that Mugabe would devastate the country to the extent that he has. He is building links with China, but meanwhile his fellow countrymen are reduced to poverty and starvation.

Racial tensions were never far from the surface, either in Rhodesia or its successor, Zimbabwe. On one occasion Universals, a mixed-race, largely Indian team were playing Sports Club, an essentially all-white team. There was also a white umpire. Universals were in the field and a number of confident appeals were turned down. The final straw

came when one of the Sports Club batsmen was trapped
on the back foot in front of middle stump and the result-
ing appeal for lbw again elicited a not out verdict. At this
point President Ebrahim and the Chairman called us off
the field and the match was abandoned.

Peter Chingoka, later to be Chairman of the Zimbabwe Cricket Union, was in what was a very multi-national
team and Babu Mamon was one of several useful players.
Unlike South Africa, there was no racial segregation. At
the time there was no first-class structure in Rhodesia.
They had a club system and played as Rhodesia in the
Currie Cup before the local Logan Cup competition became first-class with Zimbabwe's elevation to Test status
in 1992.

I was back in Rhodesia and South Africa in September
1974, for a tour with the International Wanderers. It was
a team based broadly on the Robins XI but strengthened
by world-class players like Barry Richards, Eddie Barlow,
Ian Chappell and Graeme Pollock with Graham McK-
enzie leading the attack. Brian Close again captained the
side. We began in Rhodesia where we won a three-day
match and four one-day matches, then on to South Africa
for a single match against Transvaal at the Wanderers. Batting at number three after Richards and Barlow, I was able
to resume where I had left off the previous year and after sharing a 150-plus partnership with Barry, went on to
make 154 to see the Wanderers to a declared total of over
400. Unfortunately it came to a sorry end when I ran out
Barry shortly after he had reached his century. We eventually won by a large margin, making it six wins out of six.

In March 1975, Derrick Robins organised a further tour to South Africa. It lacked the strength of earlier squads and this time there was no match against the full strength of a South African Invitation XI. We drew with Natal, Transvaal and Western Province, lost to Eastern Province thanks almost entirely to a century in each innings by Graeme Pollock, and twice to a President's XI thanks to a century by Eddie Barlow in the three-day match and some penetrating bowling by Barlow and Vintcent van der Bijl in the one-dayer. We did, however, manage two wins against an African XI, but more important than the results was the cementing of relationships with a section of South Africa's non-white community.

In September that year, I once again teamed up with my old school friend Mohammad Ilyas to represent 'Pakistan' in the Double Wicket Tournament in Johannesburg. I put 'Pakistan' in quotation marks because, as we were both banned for life there was no way that we could represent our country officially, but we took the view that the length of the ban was such that even AH Kardar was powerless to extend it. Other players included Ian and Greg Chappell, Tony Greig and John Shepherd. There was a South Africa team – Eddie Barlow and Barry Richards – and a Black South Africa team. There was even a pair from Israel! Mohammad and I did pretty well, although we didn't win the tournament.

Apartheid was finally dismantled in 1990 and the new rainbow nation established. The world will remember the role of Nelson Mandela in that process, and civil disobedience also played a part, but it would not have happened without some effort on the part of the Nationalist government. It is also too easy to forget that Mandela and FW de Klerk were jointly awarded the Nobel Peace Prize in 1993 'for their work for the peaceful termination of the apartheid regime and for laying the foundations of a new democratic South Africa'. It is regrettable that Derrick Robins received no honours for his contributions to world sport. He would not have anticipated the giddy heights of a Nobel Prize, but others have been appointed MBE for less.

In later years, Barry Richards took the view that those who came on this and subsequent rebel tours certainly played their part. In *Sundial in the Shade* by Andrew Murtagh, Richards says, 'All right, they were paid, possibly a lot, but the stick they got when they returned home was cruel and merciless. I take my hat off to them. They were acting out of noble sentiments, trying to do good for cricket in South Africa of all races ... Even today, the wounds have not fully healed. Collectively, they were known as "The Unforgiven". Yet they did more for integration than any politician. They were good guys and they got no credit for what they did, how they behaved and how they related to the blacks in our country.'

Barry was speaking mainly of the later tours under Mike Gatting and Lawrence Rowe which had been characterised by acrimony over finance and political demonstrations. Peter May (the journalist, not the former England cricket captain) does not regard the Robins tours as one of the 'rebel tours' in his book of that name, and although he mentions them, he places them in a separate category to the tours of the eighties when anti-apartheid movements were better organised and events more precisely targeted.

During my time, the Gleneagles Agreement discouraging Commonwealth countries from having sporting relations with South Africa was not yet in force. That came in 1977 and while it was never legally binding, it certainly caused those considering visiting the republic on sporting missions to think at least twice. Nevertheless, in the 1980s, in defiance of their government's position, touring teams from Sri Lanka, Australia, West Indies and England visited South Africa. They were all part of the process certainly, but it was the Derrick Robins and International Wanderers tours – of which I am proud to have taken part in three – that broke the ice.

PAKISTAN BOARD DECIDES

A LIFE BAN ON YOUNIS

YOUNIS AHMED

NEITHER Mr Derrick Robins nor Younis Ahmed was prepared to comment on the decision of the Pakistani Cricket Board of Control to ban Younis for life for touring South Africa with the Robins team, writes John Kennedy.

Mr Robins said flatly "No comment" when approached by newsmen late last night, and Younis declined to make any statement when I spoke to him moments after he had been given news of the Pakistani cricket board's decision.

No one will say but the non-White members of Mr Robins's team — Younis and the West Indian, John Shepherd—have been given strict instructions not to make Press statements on any controversial issues.

Younis knew the attitude of the Pakistani board to South Africa before accepting Mr Robins's invitation to tour, and the board's decision can not have come as a great surprise to him.

He holds a British passport, lives most of the year in England, where he plays for Surrey, and has been quoted as saying he no longer has ambitions of playing for Pakistan.

The board said Pakistanis attached to English county clubs had sought permission to undertake the tour but they have subsequently accepted the board's advice to reject the offer, reports Sapa-Reuter.

Younis had not sought the board's permission before undertaking the tour, the announcement added. His brother, Saeed, was subjected to a life ban by the Pakistani board last January for "irresponsible and undisciplined" behaviour during a tour of Australia. But the ban was later lifted pending an inquiry.

I returned to Surrey a non-international cricketer.

8

No Benefit

1973 saw Surrey recovering from a very poor season the year before. Certainly things could hardly been any worse. I like to think that after my winter in South Australia, I played my part in a considerable improvement, scoring almost 1,400 Championship runs at an average of 53.42, this time topping the averages as well as the aggregates and coming sixth in the national averages. New captain John Edrich saw Surrey to second place in the table. After a poor start we accelerated, winning nine of our last eleven matches, including the final six on the trot. There was still, however, no success in the limited overs competitions.

Of my own performances, *Wisden* said, 'The failure of the openers put the middle order batsmen under pressure, especially when Roope was on England duty. Fortunately, Younis Ahmed, the dashing left-handed Pakistani batsman was in sparkling form and was easily the side's leading run-getter .... He was a great inspiration and made his highest score, 155 not out, against Warwickshire at The Oval, followed by a century in each of the next two county matches against Yorkshire and Derbyshire.'

After my experiences on the hard pitches of Australia, I was now playing better off the back foot, but it had taken me a while to adjust to uncovered pitches. These were gradually phased out in the 1960s and England began to follow Australia's example where full covering had been the norm in Sheffield Shield matches since the 1920s. The history of pitch covering is long and tortuous and regulations have been concerned with how much of the pitch can be covered and the times at which it can be done, for instance full covering before a match starts, but then only limited covering until play has finished for the day. At the same time as full covering was being introduced in Australia, MCC, then the game's ruling body in England, was discouraging it, so those who played in both countries experienced very different conditions. There is a school of thought which believes that uncovered pitches call for higher skill levels in playing a sharply seaming or spinning ball.

Ray Illingworth has said that bowlers need greater skills to exploit uncovered pitches, but then again, he would, wouldn't he? He was principally a bowler. My own preference remains for hard, fast bouncy pitches with the ball coming on. If they wear and take a bit of turn on the final day, then fine, that's part of the game, but to have a match where one team bats on a dry pitch and the other on a wet or drying one makes a mockery of the game. I recall one match against Kent at Tunbridge Wells in 1978, where Kent won the toss and made over 300 on a dry pitch on the first day. It then rained overnight and on a drying pitch, Derek Underwood and off spinner Graham Johnson bowled us out twice. Very frustrating! Good batsmen need good pitches and it seemed unfair that those on the verge of contracts might have their careers cut off in their prime by having to play a few innings on rain-affected pitches. Batsmen have to be like dancers, light and quick on their feet and getting their head over the ball, watching the ball and controlling it. That's just not possible on poor pitches. There is also the very obvious advantage that covered pitches improve the chances of play.

There was criticism in the seventies that Oval pitches were slow and lifeless. That was quite justified. Things were to improve considerably under groundsman Harry Brind, whose company was always enjoyable; but before that I recall on more than one occasion Geoff Arnold coming back to the dressing room at an interval and aiming a kick at the first object to get in his way. Weaker counties would bowl medium pace at middle and off to defensive fields to frustrate batsmen into getting out. No wonder there were so many draws, that attendances were dropping and that one-day cricket was proving so attractive.

The match against Yorkshire was quite extraordinary. Against some quality bowling by Jackman who had seven for 36, Yorkshire capitulated to 60 all out. On a drying pitch in the second innings, they collapsed again to the spin of Pocock who had six for 11 in a total of 43. In between, admittedly in more friendly batting conditions, Surrey had declared on 268 for 8, of which I made 106. It was Stewart Storey's benefit match and unfortunate for him that Surrey's success deprived him of a day's play.

In the next match against Derbyshire at Chesterfield, I had another hundred; 117 in about three hours with fifteen fours. I was on a roll, registering four centuries and ten fifties in first-class matches that summer.

In his first year in the job, Edrich's captaincy came under scrutiny and a group of senior players expressed their dissatisfaction to the chairman, Raman Subba Row. I was surprised to be called in for an interview with Stuart Surridge, who was acting on behalf of the committee investigating the complaint, calling each player to the Committee Room for individual interviews. I was asked my opinion of Edrich as a captain and whether I was unhappy playing under him. I was taken aback and non-committal, saying I was not particularly impressed with his captaincy, nor particularly disappointed. In any case, one season was insufficient to judge his true capability. It was unfair to test him against the high standards set by Surridge himself and Micky Stewart. He needed time, a commodity not always granted to sports captains and managers, and certainly deserved at least another year to prove himself.

When John heard what had happened, he was quite angry and disappointed with his fellow players, saying that if they were unhappy with the way he led the side, then they should have come to him, not gone behind his back to the committee. I can't say whether the conspiring players had a replacement captain in mind. I was not part of the group and no one discussed it with me. But I had stood by my captain and was repaid not very kindly when, five seasons later, he was to play a big part in the decision to release me and not to award me a benefit.

I agree with *Wisden* that I was not as consistent in 1974, scoring only one century, against Leicestershire, but was still the county's leading run-scorer – jointly with Roope in all first-class matches, but with a clear lead in Championship matches. My average of 31.27, however, was, compared with the previous season, disappointing, but we did play on some very poor pitches, which made strokeplay difficult.

The Surrey Yearbook introduced a series of 'pen pictures', half a dozen lines or so dealing with the performances of each player in the preceding season. Arthur McIntyre wrote of me: 'It was ten years ago at the age of seventeen that he had a trial for Surrey; at that age he looked a fine left-handed bat, which time has proved. He played for Pakistan twice in 1969/70, and has since let it be known that his ambition is to play for England.'

The latter part was true. Pakistan had declined to consider me for selection following my decision to honour my contract with South Australia and my involvement with South Africa. It has been suggested that in 1974 I apologised to the Board for going to South Africa and was asked to meet the management of the Pakistan touring team then touring England. Neither is true, as evidenced by the fact that later that year I was again off to South Africa.

Saeed had now retired from Test cricket, so the objections which I had shared with him and my father five years earlier – that brother should not play against brother – were no longer valid. After what I considered to be ten successful years with Surrey I now felt I was good enough to represent my adopted country and made this known to the selectors. For whatever reason they did not agree and I was never given that opportunity.

In the 1974 Championship, Surrey had a promising start and at one stage looked to be possible contenders for the title, but fell away towards the end and finished seventh. Intikhab spent much of the season with the Pakistan touring team and Test calls deprived the county of Edrich and Arnold. There were no adequate replacements.

There was some consolation for a disappointing season in the Championship when we won the Benson and Hedges Cup, beating Leicestershire in a low scoring match at Lord's. It didn't look as though it was going to be all that low scoring when Surrey reached 168 for 6, but a Ken Higgs hat-trick followed, giving him overall figures of four for 12, and only two more runs were added. I had top scored with 43 before getting out to Ray Illingworth. Tight bowling by the Surrey attack put Leicestershire out for 143, only Robin Jackman having an economy rate of more than three, and that was 3.09. It was a tactical battle between the captains, Illingworth and John Edrich from which the latter emerged the winner and took the Gold Award.

Ironically, we had not made the best of starts in the competition, losing to Kent in the group stage before beating Essex, Sussex and Cambridge University. I had hit a purple patch with three undefeated innings of 101, 63 and 33, my only single figure score being against the students, which, as it happened, did not matter a great deal as we beat the weakest team in the group by over a hundred runs. Victories against the Roses counties then took us to a Lord's final and our first limited overs trophy. There were no more in my time.

It was in 1974 that I reached 10,000 first-class runs for Surrey, still the youngest to do so, just ahead of John Edrich and Jack Hobbs. I was 26 years and 308 days old. It is going to take some extraordinary *wunderkind* to beat that record, not because I would consider myself any more gifted than present and future cricketers, but rather because the reduced and reducing amount of first-class cricket is not going to provide the opportunity.

The Yearbook's pen picture for the 1975 season read: 'The first part of the season was a disappointing one for him, and it was only in the second half that he really showed his full potential as a batsman. There is no doubt that his latter form had a bearing on his side's contention for the Championship. Younis has spent the winter playing and coaching in Rhodesia.'

Reluctantly, I suppose I shall have to agree with that, but consoled myself with the fact that form is temporary while class is permanent and only mediocre teams and players are always at their best! Consistency had been a problem, but I think I managed to turn in one or two match-winning performances, scored over 1,300 runs and, although I had only one century, it was a big one, 183 not out at Worcester.

I was, nevertheless, still the highest first-class run scorer for the county, as I had been in six out of seven seasons. Only once had I had the top average, 55.58 in 1973. That spot was usually taken by John Edrich, and in all fairness, my chances of being leading run scorer were boosted by my having more innings, John missing a number of matches because of international duties.

This was, however, the season in which I recorded my best bowling figures – four for 10 against Cambridge University. I bowled thirteen overs in the match and the fact that I bowled only two more all season and was later to finish my career with a grand total of forty-nine wickets, around two per season, suggests that those figures are a reflection on the students' batting rather than my bowling!

The following season's pen picture, however, I thought was rather unfair: 'For a player of his ability, 1976 was a poor season for Younis. It was only at the end of the season that he scored runs consistently. Batting at the key position of number four, a player of his obvious talents and experience need to be far more consistent. For the winter he returned to his native Pakistan.'

Consistency again: well, maybe; but overall that season, though I had slipped to second (behind Graham Roope) in the aggregate list, I had averaged 42.15, finishing second, only just behind Edrich. I also had 161 in the last match of the season against Nottinghamshire. Statistics may not tell the whole story, but they rarely tell none of it.

It was not, however, a good year for the county. We finished mid-table in both the Championship and John Player League, and made an early exit to Derbyshire in the Gillette Cup. We did have a decent run in the Benson and Hedges before losing to Kent in the semi-final.

We could not blame international calls, John Edrich being discarded by England after bravely standing up to a hostile West Indian attack with Brian Close on a legendary Saturday evening at Old Trafford. For the first time in a quarter of a century, no Surrey player was selected for the winter tour. Geoff Arnold was out for much of the season with an Achilles tendon injury. Lonsdale Skinner, Robin Jackman and Ray Baker were involved in a road accident on their way to Worcester for a John Player League match. With a side hastily cobbled together at the last minute we lost by ten wickets, slipped from the top of the table and never looked like getting back again and for good measure the local planning authorities scotched plans for developing The Oval. Things could only get better in 1977.

Except they didn't. One bright spot was John Edrich going to his hundredth century, sadly in a deserted ground and at the fag end of a match which had already drifted to a draw. Derbyshire captain Eddie Barlow sportingly allowed the match to go into the extra half-hour for John to reach the milestone. It was an even more miserable season than 1976. We shared fourteenth place in the Championship, thirteenth in the John Player League, failed to reach the knockout stages in the Benson and Hedges Cup and went out in the quarter-finals of the Gillette Cup at Cardiff. Our last five wickets fell for thirty runs, leaving the Welshmen plenty of time to score the 200 required to win. Off the field, the impasse with the local authority continued. The ground remained antiquated and semi-derelict and the Secretary resigned. I was not party to all the bureaucratic ramifications, but it had become a very unhappy club, both on the field and in the corridors of power.

I had a poor season and played two 2nd XI matches this year, having played just one in each of the previous three seasons. I was to play four in 1978. Perhaps I should have seen the writing – or at least the graph – on the wall. I did, however share two century partnerships for the same wicket, the third, in the same match, against Northamptonshire at The Oval, a reprise of what we had done a couple of years earlier for the third wicket against Sussex.

By 1978 Fred Titmus, the former Middlesex and England off-spinner, had taken over the senior coaching position and he was pretty curt in viewing my prospects for the season, saying in his preview that, 'Younis will be looking to erase the memory of one of his most disappointing seasons since joining Surrey in 1965.' He was right, I was. 682 runs at 23.51 was way below the standard I had set myself.

It turned out to be one of Surrey's worst ever seasons. We finished sixteenth, narrowly avoiding the wooden spoon, and may well not have done so had Northamptonshire's final match of the season at Old Trafford not been washed out completely, denying them the opportunity of taking any points. Acrimony was never far away. Coach Fred Titmus resigned after Club Chairman Raman Subba Row set up a committee to look into Surrey's playing strength – which admittedly wasn't great at the time.

For me, it was a doubly disappointing season. Along with Alan Butcher and Ray Baker (and maybe cast in the role of candlestick maker), I was omitted from the side for a Championship fixture against Essex. I ended up playing in fourteen of the twenty-two Championship matches. Then, at the end of the season, along with Baker and Tom Hansell, I was released.

It had not been my best season, but aged thirty, I felt I still had plenty to offer. However, the decision was not mine. Officially, it was that of the Chairman of the Cricket Committee and the captain, the coach having already gone by then. Alf Gover was Chairman of the Cricket Committee; the captain was Roger Knight, a Cambridge blue, who had been unable to find a regular 1st XI place in 1970 and moved to Gloucestershire, then to Sussex. In 1978, he was brought back to Surrey to captain the side. He had been in the job for just one season and was still finding his feet. It is hard to say whether Knight was 100% behind the decision to let me go, but during my discussions with him there was never any hint that I would be shown the door.

Knight was, I thought, very much under the influence of the senior players, especially John Edrich, who remained the power behind the throne. I had always admired John as a batsman. He was one of very few in the game to record a hundred first-class centuries (I was with him at the crease for part of his innings when he got there at The Oval against Derbyshire in July 1977) and will always be remembered for that Saturday evening at Old Trafford when he withstood a fearsome onslaught from the West Indies pace attack. However, I do not feel he was in the same class as Micky Stewart as a leader or teammate. Edrich had always assured me that the county would award me a well-deserved benefit, but perhaps he was keen to have me out of the side. 1978 was his last season and it soon became clear that I too would play no more – at least, not at Surrey.

I was particularly disappointed at the way I was sacked. Nowadays, the normal practice is for a player to be summoned to a meeting, informed of the decision, thanked for his services, wished all the best for the future, and directed towards professional advice when that future might be outside the game. I received a two-line letter in a brown envelope informing me that the club had decided not to renew my contract for 1979 and wishing me well for the future. It was pretty brutal treatment. I wish I had kept that letter. It would have made a very good illustration for this book and would have provided a great example of Surrey's unprofessional behaviour. Within minutes of being received, however, it was torn up and thrown away, although I still have a pretty clear recollection of its contents.

With absolutely no hint of or reference to a benefit, it said: 'Dear Younis, This is to inform you that Surrey County Cricket Club has decided not to offer you a contract for 1979. We would like to thank you for your services and wish you well. Yours sincerely, Alf Gover.'

There are better, more humane, ways of letting people go. I never received any explanation from Gover, but I did receive a public acknowledgement from Club Chairman Raman Subba Row in the following spring's Yearbook: 'This part of the report would be incomplete without conveying the club's best wishes to three of our playing staff who will not be with us in 1979. To Younis Ahmed, Tom Hansell and Ray Baker we send our thanks for their support during their cricket career with us and we hope they will be back to see us at the Oval whenever they can. Our good wishes and our thanks go also to Fred Titmus who resigned last year, for all his efforts during a difficult period for the club.'

I felt very sore and badly let down and, almost forty years later, still do. It was very hurtful and even today I cannot work out how and why it should have happened. It was harsh treatment for a player who had served his county loyally for fourteen seasons and, in first-class and one-day cricket combined, contributed not far short of 20,000 runs.

Surrey have a reputation for not treating their players very well when their services are no longer required. Maybe they have been no worse than other counties, maybe their success has resulted in their sackings being higher profile and getting more publicity. The class divisions of the nineteenth century meant that players on the decline were treated pretty shabbily, a practice continuing well into the next century when the gentlemen/players amateur/professional distinction lasted into the sixties. Cricket was slow to follow changes that were taking place in society.

There were other instances of high-handed treatment, as in 1960, when Jim Laker's honorary memberships of Surrey and MCC were withdrawn. And for what? Not for any misbehaviour or criminal activity, but for expressing opinions in his book that the committee found distasteful, namely criticism of Surrey amateurs Peter May and Freddie Brown. Whatever happened to freedom of speech? I have lived in countries where that right – or privilege, as some would see it – recognised in the United Nations Declaration of Human Rights, is not respected.

It is sad to think that in the normally free-thinking west, it can also be ignored.

I took my case to an industrial tribunal who, in the time-honoured phrase, said that what Surrey had done was 'not cricket' but dismissed the case on a technicality, ruling that my employment was for part of the year only and could not be regarded as continuous. There was apparently a requirement for a minimum period of employment of twenty-six weeks before a claim for unfair dismissal could be entertained. Most county professionals were on less than that and therefore ineligible. I believe Bishen Bedi had a similar experience with Northamptonshire. It might be different now that players have longer contract terms – seven months or even twelve in some cases – and I think European Union Law allows the aggregation of separate periods of employment. On the other hand, I don't recall any recent claims of unfair dismissal being brought by released players, so maybe present contracts require players to sign away those rights. I don't know. I'm not really up to speed with what happens on the first-class circuit these days, but in any case, this is now and that was then and I had little option but to accept the tribunal's decision.

The tribunal also had no jurisdiction over benefits. I remained aghast that some players – for example Micky Stewart, Ken Barrington and John Edrich – with not much longer service, had two Surrey benefits, while I was not even granted one. Mike Willett, who played football for Corinthian Casuals, and Ron Tindall, who also played professionally for a number of teams, were both awarded benefits. Intikhab Alam, who joined in 1969, four years after me, was granted a benefit before I was. I would be the last to begrudge them that, but their length of service and their playing records do not begin to compare with mine. Between them they scored fewer runs than I did.

Withholding a benefit would be less important nowadays when, thanks to the impact of the Professional Cricketers Association, pay and pensions are much improved, but in the seventies, it was an important and much needed financial boost. Ten years' service was usually the norm. I had been on the books for fourteen seasons and while, for tax reasons, benefits have to be awarded rather than solicited, I felt I had done enough for the club to at least merit consideration.

The list of Surrey players who have scored more than 10,000 runs for the county numbers around forty and has some distinguished names on it, from Hobbs, Hayward and Sandham downwards. At the time I left Surrey I was twenty-third with 14,112 runs, having topped 1,000 in a season on seven occasions. I am now twenty-sixth, Mark Ramprakash, Alec Stewart and Alistair Brown having risen above me since 1978. I had 262 appearances, way behind Hobbs, Hayward, Strudwick, Sandham and Abel, but only four behind Alec Stewart and ahead of Stuart Surridge, Alistair Brown, Intikhab Alam and Graham Thorpe. Almost all, on both lists, have had a benefit, some have had two. There was no beneficiary in 1979. It would have been an ideal slot.

No one ever told me why. All walked away saying 'sorry: nothing to do with me'. It was very shabby treatment, and while I had every confidence that my ability would get me a contract with another county, it was highly unlikely that I would be able to play for them for a sufficient length of time to earn a benefit. In ten years' time I would be forty and whatever might have been the case in Jack Hobbs' day – or even Brian Close's or John Edrich's – it was highly unlikely that I would still be playing professional cricket at the age of forty in 1988.

I played my first first-class match for Surrey in 1965. After fourteen seasons, surely I deserved better. It was not Surrey's fault that I had not been able to reap the earnings of international cricket, but I thought my position might have elicited a bit of sympathy. Somewhere along the line I must have upset someone, but I am still in the dark as to who or how.

Ton-up Younis makes Surrey pay

YOUNIS ... a beautiful hundred.

by JOHN THICKNESSE

YOUNIS AHMED today made all his other efforts against Surrey — one hundred and five fifties in seven knocks since, they dispensed with him two years ago—look like half-hearted warm-ups.

In 126 minutes of sheer brilliance at the Oval, the 33-year-old left-hander made as beautiful a hundred as I expect to see all season with perfect strokes all round the ground.

It was tragic there were so few watching. Controlled yet devastating, it was an innings to be savoured containing 15 fours.

Coming in at 22 for 2, when Sylvester Clarke with two great yorkers, had bowled Glenn Turner and Phil Neale in successive overs, the former Pakistan Test player transformed the match.

Forty minutes after lunch steadily backed up by Mark Scott, a 22-year-old ex-MCC ground staff boy making his county debut, Younis, then 103 had stroked Worcestershire to 167 for two off 44 overs. And there was nothing anyone could do to keep him quiet.

In all, Younis played just two full strokes, a thinned leg-glance off Jackman just too wide for Graham Roope —standing in for the injured Jack Richards—to get a glove to, and a top edged hook off David Thomas which went for four.

The hundred—out of 136—arrived fittingly with a seemingly gentle cover-push off Clarke, so smooth and sweetly timed it would have gone for four but for Monte Lynch' 40-yard pursuit.

A glorious innings ended nine minutes and three fours later when Younis clipped Jackman to Thomas at midwicket. Worcester were then 175 for three and the third wicket stand was worth 153 off 36 overs.

● County scoreboard—Page 32.

I may have derived a little satisfaction from this innings!

9

Three Pears

Given my acrimonious departure, I wanted to get as far away from The Oval as possible. I couldn't have gone much further.

I had enjoyed life my single season in Adelaide with South Australia in 1972/73 and made some wonderful friends there, so I did not take much persuading to take up an East Torrens contract which I was offered for the 1978/79 season. From the beginning of the grade competition in Adelaide in the late nineteenth century, East Torrens have been one of the leading clubs and have won it more than any other.

It was an interesting season. Despite being released by Surrey, I was still confident in my ability both as a player and a coach and was able to offer something to the younger players of the club. They ran four sides with well-attended nets on Tuesday and Thursday evenings and a coach for each net. It was a useful season for me both in terms of my personal performance and my development as a coach. East Torrens were a good side; team spirit was very good, both on and off the field, and we made the finals of the grade competition. Australian grade cricket is no less intense than state cricket. I have always admired and enjoyed the way they play. They don't like losing. Not a bad thing at all.

Gloria was pregnant when she travelled to the other side of the world with me, and our daughter, Yasmine, was born in Adelaide on 16 January 1979. Together with three-year-old Sam, we were now a family of four – but not for long.

My mind was still partly in England. I had no intention of giving up the county game. I was still only thirty-one and felt I had a few years in me yet, although without any firm idea of where I would be playing my cricket in the summer of 1979. I had not approached any counties, but I did not have to wait long. I received a number of offers, the most attractive of which was a two-year contract with Worcestershire. I was looking forward to returning to first-class cricket in England and playing with a new county, though I realised that living and playing in Worcester, a small provincial city quite different from London, would be a new experience. My home ground would no longer be The Oval, but New Road, about as big a contrast as can be imagined. On the outskirts of the city, it is among the more attractive county grounds with the cathedral forming an impressive backdrop. It helped that the pitch was very similar to the Campbelltown Oval where I had been playing for East Torrens.

The Worcesterians were very friendly people, both at the club and in the city. I was welcomed by captain Norman Gifford and coach Basil D'Oliveira and felt at home immediately. For the latter I had tremendous admiration, both as a player – an aggressive batsman and as a medium pace bowler, a master of swing, seam and accuracy – and for the dignity he demonstrated when he became a political pawn in the D'Oliveira affair of 1968. I was to call him Sir Basil. I had played against most of the Worcestershire team for Surrey and had no difficulty in slotting into a happy and united but purposeful dressing room.

At the first meeting Norman announced that he and the team were looking forward to seeing me hit the ball all round the park. It meant a lot that the club had confidence in me and I would do my best to justify it. If the captain is unsure whether they have signed the right player, then it is a different ball game. Fortunately, that was not the case. I justified that confidence and was awarded my county cap after only one season.

I was at ease with players like Alan Ormrod around and a nice, hard bouncy track to bat on. My first season was an outstanding success for both myself and the county. It was a strong-looking side with Norman Gifford as captain and Glenn Turner as an accumulator of big runs.

My first Championship match was against Somerset at New Road. It was not without controversy. The start was delayed until the afternoon session because the starting handle for the heavy roller had somehow detached itself and been squashed by the weight of the machine into the pitch on a length. The pitch was remown and the stumps moved a few feet to allow the match to progress. I made

52, some of them against Joel Garner who used his height effectively to get a bit of bounce and take eight for 60 in the innings. I was on the way. What I had done for Surrey was irrelevant. This was a new club, a new start and I was lucky that things had gone my way in my first match.

There was further and more acrimonious controversy with Somerset when we met them later in the season in a Benson and Hedges match. The format of the competition was one of four groups, the top two in each to progress to the quarter finals. Brian Rose, the Somerset captain, had worked out that he could afford to lose a match and still progress to the semi-provided he preserved Somerset's run rate, which would act as a tie-breaker should the final group table result in two teams being on the same points. Aware of this, Brian declared the innings closed after one over with the total at 1 for 0, the one being a no ball from Vanburn Holder. It took Worcestershire two overs to pass that total and the match was over. Somerset had lost but still qualified for the quarter-finals, leaving a small crowd completely bemused and unaware of what was going on. Even the Somerset players could not believe what had happened and were so embarrassed they did not know what to say or do. Fleet Street descended on New Road. It was a very sad day for cricket.

Worcestershire and mathematics had won; Somerset and the spirit of the game had lost. There were rumours before the match that something of the kind might happen, but we assumed it was just a ploy to wind us up, trying to make us expect a declaration after one over but having to field for another 54. Those who had paid for admission expected – not unreasonably – to see a day's cricket. They had their entrance fee refunded. Somerset were thrown out of the competition and a new playing condition was added to those of limited overs cricket, prohibiting declarations.

Worcestershire were never very far from controversy that summer, although another incident involving a declaration was of a more innocent kind and arose from ignorance of the laws. In the match against Northamptonshire at New Road, the first day was washed out completely. Having bowled out our opponents for 294, in an attempt to force a result, Norman Gifford declared at 146 for 6, having avoided the follow on. Except he hadn't. The match had been reduced to two days with the consequence that the lead required to enforce the follow on was no longer 150, but 100. Northamptonshire captain, Patrick Watts, was a little more clued up on the laws and invited Worcestershire to bat again. It was an invitation they were in no position to refuse. Fortunately, Alan Ormrod and Phil Neale had no difficulty batting out time.

Then there was the occasion at Derby when Worcestershire bowled out Derbyshire with very little time left and were told they had four overs to make 25 to win. However, as the players took the field, a phone call to Lord's ascertained that there were only two overs remaining. We ended on 17 for 1. With four overs we would almost certainly have got there. Two made it doubly difficult.

I had a great partnership with Glenn Turner. We scored heavily in all four competitions. I had seven centuries that season and, with just short of 70, was second to Geoffrey Boycott in the first-class averages. Despite his obvious superiority to the rest of the team, Glenn was always one of the boys, a great storyteller and excellent company off the field. He was very approachable and while he would never impose his opinions, he was always willing to give advice when asked. He had a tremendous knowledge of the game and, in addition to his batting skills, was an outstanding slip fielder. It was interesting to watch his own development: when I first came across him, he hardly hit the ball off the square and would be about 20 not out after two and a half hours batting. But later he expanded his range of attacking shots to become one of the fastest scorers on the county circuit and was up there with the world's best.

A very special innings for me that year was the 221 not out against Nottinghamshire at Trent Bridge. The home side had, as usual, prepared a green top for what was perhaps one of the best seam attacks in the world, Richard Hadlee and Clive Rice. We batted first, having lost the toss, in a heavy atmosphere and under low cloud. The two superstars soon made inroads: Glenn Turner went for a duck to Richard Hadlee, two more wickets followed quickly and we stood at 41 for 3.

Alan Ormrod and I then added 281 runs, a fourth wicket record for the county. My plan was to bat through the overs and get a double hundred. By lunch I was around 60 not out, I had my hundred by tea. I was by now well set and, had it not been for the first innings restriction of 100 overs, might well have had more than my eventual 221 not out. It was one of my best innings against some very good bowlers. Off spinner Eddie Hemmings and left-arm spinner Michael Bore, recently acquired from Yorkshire, were more than adequate to follow up Hadlee and Rice. Their plan had been to put us in, bowl us out cheaply, run up a big score, then bowl us out again. It didn't quite work out like that. In the end, we had a decent lead on first innings and ended up winning by 49 runs, one of seven victories that season which took us to second place in the Championship table, having been fifteenth the previous season. I felt I was beginning to make a difference to the team.

Centuries – double ones in particular – are special, but statistics in isolation are often meaningless. You have to ask against whom the runs were made and in what circumstances. To both those questions it was, on this occasion, very gratifying to be able to give answers which satisfy not only the statisticians, but also those who judge the merits of an innings from a non-statistical standpoint.

Two of my centuries were against Surrey, the first in the Benson and Hedges Cup at Worcester and then in the Championship at Guildford. Surrey, now with Micky Stewart as manager, were having a better season and ended up third just behind Worcestershire. I felt I had something to prove against them. I had no antagonism towards the players nor, I think, they towards me, but I was still feeling sore about the way I was dismissed and their failure to give me a benefit. Anger and frustration were still there, but I was able to channel them into a more acute concentration. So I guess I approached the matches in a similar way to that in which I would have done a Test match.

I received the Gold Award for my Benson and Hedges innings, but as a team, we did not score enough and Surrey beat us with five overs to spare. That was disappointing, but we compensated by a nine-wicket win at Guildford.

It might have been different if Sylvester Clarke and Robin Jackman had not been sidelined through injury, but it was nevertheless highly satisfying to be at the crease when we hit the victory target, to shake hands with former colleagues and to walk off to the applause of Surrey supporters and members who, I would like to think, were coming to appreciate what they had been missing.

I seem to have had a habit of getting into the record books in Surrey v Worcestershire matches, at least those pages which deal with the highest partnerships for each wicket for both teams. The seventh-wicket partnership of 173 which I shared with Intikhab at Worcester in 1975 still stands, though the 194 I had with Graham Roope for the fourth wicket at The Oval in 1972 has gone, bettered by Mark Ramprakash and Alistair Brown who added 229 at Worcester in 2006. Likewise, the 153 for the third wicket I shared with Mark Scott was eclipsed at Whitgift School by the 223 compiled by Vikram Solanki and Moeen Ali in 2010.

The dressing room atmosphere was totally different from what I had been experiencing the last two or three years at Surrey, where there had been plots and sub-plots and people knifing one another in the back. Here it was totally pleasant with everyone talking to everyone else and genuinely working together as a team. We were pleased when one of our teammates did well: Surrey players pretended to be, but underneath there was resentment at others' success.

It was always a good experience to sit round with the Worcestershire players in the evening, after a day's play, sharing reminiscences and experiences of playing in different parts of the world. It was effortless bonding, united by a love of the game and confirmed to me, if it needed confirming, that I was still playing pretty well, benefiting from previous experiences and still had a few years left in me – almost another decade as it turned out.

In October came the welcome news that, after being in force for six years, my life ban had been lifted by the Pakistan board, though I suspect the decision was more to do with my successful season than any political change of heart. So from 1980, I would be free to play for England or Pakistan. My ambitions had turned towards England, but of course I had to be selected first – a decision for others to take.

I was delighted. It is never a nice feeling to be banned from anything, and while the decision to impose a life-time ban would have had its supporters, it was taken by one autocrat and no opportunity was ever afforded me to state my case. A number of people in Pakistan, as well as Pakistanis living in England, had said to me that they would have loved to see me in the Pakistan squad and shared my view that I had been unjustly treated and should have been given an opportunity to defend my actions. If England did not want me, I now had a second string to my bow.

However, not everything was positive at this stage of my life – after nine years of marriage, Gloria and I were divorced. Gloria loved Adelaide and wanted to settle there, but I still had a cricket career to follow which took me to other parts of the world. In legal terms, under the Matrimonial Causes Act, the reason had to be irretrievable breakdown. The reality, however, was very different.

We split on very amicable terms with no acrimony and no mud-slinging. The life of a professional cricketer and marriage do not mix very well. In addition to overseas tours, half the domestic fixtures are played away. At the time I played, more so than today, after-play socialising with one's colleagues and the opposition was very much the norm. I saw very little of home and a parting of the ways with Gloria was the perhaps inevitable consequence. She has never remarried, but took on the responsibility of bringing up the children, then aged five and one, in the Islamic faith. She fulfilled all my expectations and we have remained on exceptionally good terms.

Sir Donald Bradman was once again very kind and through his contacts and advice I was able to arrange my children's education at Pembroke College, one of Adelaide's leading schools where John Inverarity, former Western Australia and Australia cricketer was Headmaster, only a street away from Sir Donald's house. It is a school with a strong sporting reputation, particularly in cricket and Australian Rules Football. Sam excelled and captained school teams at both sports, had a trial for South Australia and later joined the Australian Cricket Academy under the direction of Rodney Marsh. He was a seam bowler and opening bat and has played for a number of county 2nd XIs, as well as for Morpeth in the Northumberland County League. As his father, I'm probably biased, but I always thought he was good enough to play professional cricket. However, it is no longer possible these days to pursue simultaneously a career in professional sport and a career in business. He went to Johannesburg and Cape Town where he impressed Duncan Fletcher, Western

Province Head Coach at the time, before going to Malaysia to play and coach cricket. He stayed in the area and is now Senior Vice-President of MasterCard in Singapore. Equipped with his Harvard MBA, he has become a successful businessman and has said to me, 'Dad, what you earned in twelve years at Surrey, I have earned in two. There's the reason for switching from cricket to business!'

My daughter, Yasmine, did equally well in school and is now an international lawyer. She worked for the Foreign Office in Whitehall and is now Director of a Law Company in London. I am very proud of both her and Sam, as I am of my other son, Cyrus, now living and working in Spain. I am also a grandfather to two boys and two princesses.

I returned to Worcester for the 1980 season and began the process of familiarising myself with local conditions once again. I've always said that batting on the fast true wickets of Australia helped my technique, particularly shots off the back foot, but coming back to a cold, damp England with leaden skies and green pitches which were a paradise for the seamers required a period of adjustment, a tightening of the game and playing the ball as late as possible. Batting with Glenn Turner made that a lot easier. By the time I got in he'd usually given the side a good start and I needed less time to play myself in against a ball that had lost its initial shine.

The season was not as successful as 1979 had been, either for me or for the club. We finished lower in the Championship and in the John Player League, but we improved our performance in the Benson and Hedges and Gillette Cups, reaching the semi-finals and quarter-finals respectively. I struggled in the early part of the season but improved towards the end with a couple of centuries against Warwickshire at Edgbaston and Nottinghamshire at Cleethorpes. I was third in the Championship averages, but at 38.96 was still some way behind Turner and Ormrod. My most significant innings in the first part of the season was the 113 I had against Yorkshire. It partly cancelled out Geoffrey Boycott's 142 and enabled us to chase down the Tykes' total with an over and four wickets to spare.

At the end of the season Norman Gifford announced his retirement from the captaincy, though he would stay on as a player while Glenn Turner took the reins. Under the new captain it was very much a season of two halves. Injuries and the weather did not help and we made a dreadful start, but finished with a flourish. My own performance was much more even – 'powerful ease' said *Wisden* – and Ormrod, Turner and I all finished with batting averages over 50.

That season I had 116 against Surrey at The Oval, an innings which received a few comments in the national press, although maybe less for the innings than for the fact that I had upset The Oval hierarchy by parking my sponsored Porsche in the place designated for the Chairman of Marketing, rather than the less prestigious and less convenient ones allocated to visiting players!

It has been suggested that I was a prickly and abrasive player and had a fiery nature. That is for others to judge. I would say that I was always intensely competitive and gave my all for whichever team I played for. Occasionally I may have overstepped the mark. It is said that on being given out at Chesterfield in 1981 I kicked over the stumps... that I do not remember, but I do recall questioning a wide called by David Evans in the John Player League match against Hampshire the following Sunday. I went to the umpires' room at tea time and apologised. My apology was accepted.

An innovation in 1981 was the seven-a-side 10-over floodlit competition towards the end of the season, sponsored by the cigarette company Lambert and Butler. It was played at The Hawthorns, the ground of West Bromwich Albion Football Club and other clubs elsewhere in the country. It was too novel and did not last.

The 1982 season was one of transition. Norman Gifford had finally retired while Glenn Turner relinquished the captaincy and had his season curtailed by an appendix operation at the end of July. Phil Neale took over as captain, but his early season training was affected by his football commitments with Lincoln City.

Our young 2nd XI won their Championship, recalling for me memories of when Surrey had done the same in 1966 and laid the foundations for the 1st XI Championship win of 1971. Worcestershire was similar, winning the County Championship six years later in 1988 and 1989. Not precisely the same players, but perhaps the same team spirit and a few names due to become better known in later years: Damian D'Oliveira, Mike Weston, Richard Illingworth and Vanburn Holder. For most of July I was out of the game through a neck injury, but I was delighted to help the 2nd XI out on a couple of occasions.

Nevertheless, the bulk of my cricket was with the 1st XI. I managed three centuries that season, a Championship average of 47.22 and, despite missing a month of the season, still got past the thousand run mark. I was in a good place and looked forward to helping the county to success and trophies in the years ahead. Unfortunately it was not to happen.

Glenn Turner left the club, partly in frustration at the TCCB's new restriction on overseas players which meant that he and Hartley Alleyne could not play in the same fixture. He did not go, however, before playing one of the most remarkable innings it has been my privilege to witness. His hundredth century was amazing, even by his own standards. I had batted for a while with John Edrich a few years earlier when he had achieved the same target, but this was something special. One century was not enough. He went on to score a second and then a third, a century before lunch, another one between lunch and tea and a few more in the evening, allowing us to declare and have a few overs at our opponents before the close. It was against Warwickshire at New Road, our near neighbours, and always a bit of a needle match, though I have to say that while there might have been acrimony among supporters and members, there was no antagonism between the players. Worcestershire eventually declared with the total on 501 for 1 and Glenn 311 not out. I had sat with my pads on all day and didn't get on the park before Worcestershire went out to field.

Boosted by that remarkable innings, Glenn managed almost as many Championship runs as I did, and he played in only eight matches. An undefeated double century against Oxford University earlier in the season took his average to over 90 and a place at the top of the national list, twenty runs per innings ahead of second-placed Zaheer Abbas.

Towards the end of 1982 I had the privilege (if that's the right word!) of being in the batting order that, despite the bowling of Malcolm Marshall, squeezed home by one wicket against Hampshire at Southampton. Marshall had taken career-best bowling figures of eight for 71 in the first innings and was rampant in the second. Two wickets had gone early.

Off the field, Malcolm was one of the nicest and mildest mannered men in the game. On the field, it was a different story. He was a professional cricketer with a job to do. He was at his best that day and bowled me at least half a dozen consecutive bouncers. He had the knack of bowling a full length for two or three balls to draw the batsman on to the front foot, then unleashing his bouncer as a surprise weapon. Sometimes he would bowl a bouncer or two, then with the batsman on the back foot would unleash an often wicket-taking yorker, not dealt with in the most effective fashion from the back foot! He was one of the finest quick bowlers I faced in my career, combining pace with accuracy and capable of swinging the ball both ways.

Marshall wanted my wicket early. I took balls on the arms and body. Words were exchanged. At time the pain was excruciating, but with the Brian Close mantra of 'it only hurts if you think it does' in my mind, I did my best not to show it. In later years the number of fast short-pitched balls were limited to one or two per over, but at this time there was no such restriction. There were, however, laws on intimidatory bowling which on this (and several other) occasions the umpires weakly failed to enforce. I was very disappointed with them.

At the end of play, Malcolm the gentleman took over. He was the first in to our dressing room to ask whether I was all right. He was one of a group of devastating West Indian fast bowlers. There were others in other parts of the world through the eighties and nineties, as helmets began to appear on the scene, and now it is rare to see a batsman at the crease without one. Sadly, Malcolm was taken from us all too early, dying of cancer of the colon at the young age of forty-one.

I had enjoyed my four years with Worcestershire, but things came crashing down in 1983 when my season ended almost before it started. I was accused of placing a bet on Leicestershire to beat Worcestershire in a John Player League match in early May. It was all a sad misunderstanding. Let me give my side of the story. During a rain-affected match at Worcester, I had gone for a three-mile run. There's plenty of opportunity to do that at New Road, with King's School playing fields next door, open country at the Diglis End and a path along the River Severn. There was so much rain around that it was almost certain there would be no play and sure enough, play was called off at lunchtime.

Feeling pretty well exhausted, I showered, relaxed on one of the benches in the dressing room and fell half asleep, only to be awakened by Paul Pridgeon, one of several horse racing enthusiasts in the side (all counties have one or two of them) collecting bets for whatever race meetings were taking place that day. I know next to nothing about horses and horse racing, so I declined the offer. He then said it didn't have to be horses. I could bet on anything I liked, including cricket. All right, I said, put £100 on Leicestershire to beat us in the John Player League. I then went back to sleep having launched a dressing room joke which spectacularly backfired.

The next thing I knew I was woken up by the dressing room attendant who told me that Chairman Duncan Fearnley wished to see me in the office. He came straight to the point, saying he said he could scarcely believe what he had heard, that I had placed a large bet against my own team. Neither could I scarcely believe it – a light-hearted joke had been taken seriously. Even harder to believe was that Pridgeon had gone to Phil Neale, the Worcestershire captain, to inform him of what I had said. I believe that Phil Neale then decided to go to the chairman, who was at the ground to watch the match.

I feel this was not the right thing to do – he should have spoken to me first – and I am still disappointed with the way he handled it. The captain had failed in what I saw as his moral duty, to find out from me what had happened before speaking to the chairman. He knew full well that I am not a betting person and would never look to make money placing a bet on a cricket match. In my opinion, it was the actions of a weak and gutless captain.

As I explained to the chairman, if I had really wanted to place a bet on the match, I would not have done it in front of all my teammates. There were several book-makers in the city and it would have been no problem to go across the bridge during my run and put a bet on. Furthermore, I reminded the Chairman that a number of players in the dressing room loved putting bets on horses, but I was not one of them. He was not impressed by the argument, telephoned a few members of the committee and persuaded them to share his views, then referred the matter to the full committee. I was asked to put my side of the story and, after I had done so, it was decided to cancel my contract.

Until this point, I had always had a pretty amicable relationship with Duncan Fearnley, appearing in programmes in advertisements for his company's cricket equipment. For that, incidentally, I am still awaiting payment. It has now gone into the not-going-to-happen file, along with my Surrey benefit.

So, no more cricket that summer. I suppose I might have picked up a contract somewhere, with a northern league club perhaps, but most would have made their arrangements by this time and having played first-class cricket for so long, club cricket would have been something of an anti-climax. I put my gear away, packed my bags and took myself off to Adelaide, my children and an Australian winter, often warmer than an English summer. It was time to watch my son play Australian Rules Football rather than play my own cricket.

My marriage to Puchi – a happy partnership.

10

A Welcome in Wales

Due to the unseemly end of my time at Worcestershire, I was already in Australia as clubs began their preparations for the 1983/84 season. I had had conversations with one or two clubs, but nothing materialised. Much as I enjoyed Adelaide and East Torrens, I thought I might enjoy living and playing in a bigger city like Melbourne or Sydney. When I received a very generous offer from East Malvern to coach and play there, on the outskirts of Melbourne in the Victoria District competition, it was a simple decision to say yes.

East Malvern were financed by a multi-millionaire, Rob McAfee, and they offered a very generous contract. I played two seasons there, in 1983/84 and 1984/85. I was provided with a penthouse suite on the St Kilda Road, a stone's throw from the Melbourne Cricket Ground and overlooking the city. Mr McAfee had bought it for investment purposes with a view to selling at a profit in the future, but in the meantime he let me have use of it. Several other overseas first-class cricketers had come to play, including West Indians Desmond Haynes and Hartley Alleyne. There was a lot of high-class cricket and the social scene was also very good.

Melbourne is a big city, one of the finest in the world, with lots of money around. The hospitality in people's homes was fantastic and I had a great time there. The Melbourne Cup was special. People come from all over Australia and indeed all over the world and the nation comes to a halt while the race is being run. It is a very special day and everyone has a fantastic time, especially those who benefit from a bit of corporate hospitality.

I have always enjoyed the company of Australians, the outdoor life and the hard way they play their cricket. They don't enjoy losing, but then again, they don't have much experience of it. They give 110% on the field but usually enjoy a few beers afterwards.

East Malvern was a great experience, but it wasn't first-class cricket. By the end of my first season, having played no first-class cricket since my abrupt departure from Worcestershire a year or so earlier but still in my mid-thirties, I felt I had a few more years in me. In fact, I felt I was playing better cricket than ever and I was enjoying myself. I was certainly not ready to retire and thought I had still something to offer to the game I loved.

From Australia, I had been in negotiations with Ken Taylor, Cricket Manager at Nottinghamshire. Trent Bridge was a lucky ground where I hardly ever failed. Somehow or other I had managed to score runs against Notts most times I played against them and they were very keen to have me. There had even been a possibility that I might join Nottinghamshire in 1982. They were looking to strengthen the squad by the addition of a left-handed middle-order batsman to help retain the Championship they had won the previous season, but the deal did not get off the ground as I was still contracted to Worcestershire.

I was on the verge of signing a contract with Nottinghamshire when I was approached by Glamorgan with a particularly attractive offer. Mike Selvey had been released by Middlesex and was to join Glamorgan as captain. He had heard in London that I was on the market.

I received a call from Phil Carling, whom I had known from my early days in England when he was a schoolboy in New Malden playing for Malden Wanderers and later Cambridge University. He had had trials with Surrey and played a few 2nd XI matches but did not succeed in securing a contract. After Cambridge, he followed a path in cricket administration which had led him to the post of Secretary at Glamorgan County Cricket Club. Mike Selvey informed him that he would very much like to bring in new players and was anxious to add an experienced middle-order batsman to the squad. Phil rang me, saying that Glamorgan were keen to have a chat with me before I signed with Nottinghamshire. I informed him I was on the verge of doing so, but he was persistent and asked that I considered delaying the Nottinghamshire deal to give Glamorgan the chance of putting an offer on the table. I agreed and met Phil in London on my return. He travelled from South Wales and we met at Paddington station, where he brandished an offer already typed out and ready to sign. In financial terms, it was better than what Nottinghamshire had in mind, but I did not want to make an instant decision and asked for time to consider.

It was not a question of money, but of choosing the right county. I consulted friends and family; Phil travelled to London again a couple of days later so we could discuss the finer details. I was influenced by the fact that Javed Miandad, a tough character whom I greatly admired, was already at Glamorgan. Mike Selvey had an astute cricket brain and was of the opinion that my presence would make a difference. Three years, decent money, a three-bedroom house and car, £1 per run in all competitions and an extra bonus for making five or more centuries in a season all added to the attraction. That compared well with Nottinghamshire's offer of a two-year contract with no similar incentives. I was made to feel very welcome in Glamorgan; I enjoyed the atmosphere and playing along-side Javed, and made a decent if not over-spectacular contribution of just over 1,000 runs at an average of just under 40.

I was happy to make a century on debut for my new county – 154 not out against Oxford University in The Parks. A defeat by Middlesex followed and then a satisfactory win at New Road against Worcestershire, coinciding almost exactly with the anniversary of my dismissal.

So I was feeling pretty confident when I stepped out for my first match in the John Player League for Glamorgan at St Helen's, Swansea. It was against Gloucestershire and I was batting pretty well. I had made 34 and had just taken the score through 200 with a couple of drives off David (Syd) Lawrence. Syd was a lovely guy – unless he had a cricket ball in his hand. The score triggered a typical fast bowler's reaction. The next ball was a bouncer which I went to hook and missed. It was the end of my participation in the match. There was blood everywhere. I was helped from the field to a waiting ambulance; shortly afterwards, I was in hospital with a broken jaw. Swansea has, I believe, more steps from the playing area to the dressing rooms than any other first-class ground in the UK. The locals reckon about a hundred. I don't know, I've never counted them, but that day it seemed like three times more. At the hospital I received no sympathy from a martinet of a nurse who regarded any sports injury (and as St Helen's doubles as a rugby venue, she must have seen a few) as self-inflicted. Helmets had just begun to come on to the cricket scene in the late 1970s and were not as ubiquitous as they have subsequently become.

Thankfully, the broken jaw didn't stop a new relationship blossoming. It was about this time that I met Puchi, who was to become my second wife. We met in London, having been introduced through a mutual friend who said that I would like her. Born in Kenya but with family roots in the Punjab, Puchi spoke Punjabi and Urdu and had business interests in fashion, property and catering. The fact that we have now been happily married for thirty years and that Puchi treats my children as her own is testimony to the accuracy of our friend's prediction. She has a great personality, is a wonderful cook and her Pakistani and Punjabi cuisine, along with her ability in South African, Australian and Mediterranean specialities, have helped us establish a worldwide circle of friends.

Unfortunately, Mike Selvey had a disastrous time as Glamorgan captain and did not survive long, giving way to Rodney Ontong halfway through the following season. Mike didn't seem to have a clue about what was required and lost the dressing room.

Rodney was a great improvement. He had a good cricketing brain, he was a fighter with sound batting technique and taught himself to bowl very useful off spin, which at times he used to good effect – not always the case with bowling captains, some of whom tend either to underbowl or overbowl themselves. When I played against him for Surrey he was a middle-order batsman and mediumpace bowler, but he was an intelligent cricketer who could adapt his game to the circumstances. I thought he was very unlucky not to get the nod from England. His all-round ability would certainly have improved the options but, perhaps because Glamorgan was regarded as an unfashionable county, he was never considered by the England selectors. He was always a team player. He shared my view that the success of the team was all important and that personal performances were secondary.

Rodney Ontong was a good captain, but the undoubted star was my countryman Javed Miandad. I had always admired Javed as a cricketer, a tenacious and determined personality and a great thinker on the game. In the early part of his career he was also a useful leg spinner, but problems with his back meant that he soon abandoned that aspect of his game to concentrate on his batting, which would become world class. His stance was unorthodox and two-eyed, but he was able to pick the length uncannily early and, until Younus Khan took his record recently, was Pakistan's highest Test run scorer. Javed was not universally popular and he had a justified reputation for speaking his mind. He was also notorious for his on-field confrontation with Dennis Lillee during the Australia-Pakistan Test at Perth in 1981.

Javed has something of a reputation as a street fighter. He was a muhajir, one of many who moved to Karachi from Uttar Pradesh, Bihar and Delhi after Partition, and epitomised the mentality described by Osman Saliuddin: 'In a way, muhajirs represent the idea of Pakistan as it was conceived, believers of the original dream. They moved here to prosper economically in a way they felt wasn't possible in India, To some, maybe many of them, Pakistan was a world of opportunity first and a citadel of Islam second ... Their plan of life is simple and universal; get an education, find a job, work hard, be somebody, educate your children and repeat.' It was an aspirational approach to life which I greatly admired. Not everyone did.

I played both with and against Javed and first met him when he played for Sussex, but this was the first time I really got to know him. He became a great friend. Puchi's cooking helped. She would travel from London on a Friday evening and the following day cook enough food to fill the freezer and last the following week, although with Javed around, it rarely did.

Puchi was there to witness my record stand with Javed against the Australians at Neath in 1985. It was the custom for Glamorgan to entertain the tourists twice a year over the bank holiday weekends, but that tradition has now gone as the intensive programme of internationals make it impossible for touring teams to play more than one or two counties – most do not see them at all. This one was played in July, a break from normal practice.

Normally the matches were played at Cardiff or Swansea, but the Neath Borough Council and Neath Development Partnership had sponsored the match to the extent of £20,000 and Glamorgan's financial decision-makers had decided that the resultant lower gate receipts caused by the lower capacity were more than counterbalanced by the size of the sponsorship. That was no concern of Javed's or mine, however, we were just happy to enjoy a pleasant ground with, on this occasion certainly, a very sound batting surface.

Anyway, Javed and I enjoyed ourselves. I had spent time in Australia, coaching and playing state and grade cricket, and admired their attitude to the game. Javed had his famous spat with Dennis Lillee and I had had a few run-ins with Australian cricketers, born of a passion for the game on both sides. I knew the match would be reported in the Australian media and wished to impress Ian Chappell, who had never wanted me, and Sir Donald Bradman, who had backed me and proved so helpful during my time in Adelaide. So the adrenalin was flowing before the partnership began.

Jeff Thompson was playing, as was Greg Matthews and a couple of other useful bowlers; slow left armer Murray Bennett, who took the three wickets to fall, and David Gilbert, later to be Cricket Manager at Surrey and Chief Executive of the New South Wales Cricket Association. We began at 103 for 3 and eventually declared at 409 for 3 when Javed completed his double century with a six over extra cover. Both of us were determined not to get out. It confirmed that I could play a bit. On the other side of the world, Sir Donald picked up the news and conveyed his congratulations to my ex-wife Gloria in Adelaide. There were telegrams of congratulation from my children, Sam and Yasmine, and a few happy tears were shed.

A number of records were broken. Javed's innings was the highest for Glamorgan against a touring side. The partnership was a record for the county's fourth wicket and the highest for any wicket against a touring team. Javed's fourth double century was a record for the county, it was the first occasion two Glamorgan players had scored centuries in the same match against the tourists and for good measure the highest individual innings and highest team total for a first-class match on the ground.

I was awarded my third county cap and topped the averages that year. Javed was second and Rodney Ontong third; all of us were above 50. It was an indication of the extent to which Glamorgan in those days relied on overseas players. The first Welshman on the list was Hugh Morris, some way down.

We didn't just try to outdo the Welshmen at cricket. Javed and I would often sing in the showers at Sophia Gardens. The pavilion, now demolished to make way for the new SWALEC stadium, was quite small and the noise would drift up to the balcony, no doubt much to the consternation of Glamorgan members. The Welsh pride themselves on the quality of their music and it was pretty certain on the basis of our performance that we would not be invited to audition for any of the many male voice choirs in the principality.

I was back to singing as a soloist the following year when Javed – always a law unto himself, and even by Pakistani standards not the best organised – failed to report until halfway through the season and had his contract terminated. Rodney Ontong, who had not wished to continue as captain beyond the end of the season, brought forward his resignation and handed over to Hugh Morris. John Steele, now retired from playing, was appointed as Assistant Secretary with special responsibilities as advisor to the captain.

The disruption had an impact on the playing field and Glamorgan finished bottom of the Championship by some distance. Only on two occasions since winning it in 1969 had they made the top ten, but this was only the second occasion that they held the wooden spoon. All four matches in the Benson and Hedges were lost; a mere half dozen wins in the John Player League ensured a place in the lower half of the table and the sole victory in the NatWest Bank Trophy was against Staffordshire of the Minor Counties. Only Hugh Morris had 1,000 Championship runs.

I topped the averages with just over 40, but I had now played twenty-two seasons in county cricket and was getting tired of the travelling, the impersonal hotels, reporting to the ground every day. I spoke to Phil Carling and we agreed to part company. There would be no extension of my contract. Ironically, however, I was to be given another opportunity to play Test cricket.

So ended my first-class career in England and Wales. Looking back on it, like a good wine, I improved with age. My batting average with Glamorgan had been just under 50, with Worcestershire just over. For Surrey it had been 36.65. Forty is about the standard that players look for, so while those figures might support Surrey's decision to discontinue my contract, they might also mean that Surrey missed out on my best years. Of course, averages can be very misleading and distorted by the odd big innings or a number of not outs, so perhaps a fairer comparison would be the number of centuries scored. For Surrey this was nineteen in 448 innings – about one in every twenty-three, while for Worcestershire and Glamorgan combined it was twenty-one – about one in every ten.

Looking back on my performances against each opponent, I see there was some support for Ken Taylor's theory that I always did well against his county. I averaged 53.94 against Nottinghamshire, but better than that were 60.66 against Surrey where I was always determined to do well. Against Warwickshire, Worcestershire's great local rivals, it was 65.92 with a century every six innings.

A lot of batting is in the mind. It seems I always did better when I had a point to prove.

V
928116 PO EM G
OSEAGRAM K1 LN

G575 CHC850 VS8732 LD104
GBXX HL PWKX 015
LAHORE 15 6 1445 DLVR 7TH

LT
YOUNAS AHMED STEPPYING STONE 24 HESSLE GROVE
EPSOM

BAN LIFTED BY PAKISTAN GOVT
PAKCRICKET

COL 24

OSEAGRAM K1 LN
928116 PO FM GO

EPSOM
TELEGRAMS
6 OCT 1979

-7 OCT.79

889321 PO BV G
OSEAGRAM 30 LN
Q1 ELB8316 QSA930 LIF215
GBXX CO PWKX 012
LAHORE 12/10 6 2150

INAYATLLAH
65 KINGSTON ROAD
AMBLEDON SW19 LONDON

CONGRATULTIONS BAN LIFTED
ZULFIQAR

COL 19 65

889321 PO BV G
OSEAGRAM 30 LN

The happy news that I was no longer exiled from
international cricket came via telegram.

11

Seventeen Years

With my three-year contract with Glamorgan over, I went back to Pakistan and captained Lahore City, scoring a century in my first match against United Bank.

In the team was a promising twenty-year-old in the shape of Aamer Sohail. He looked good in the nets and in the middle but had an irritating habit of doing the hard work, seeing off the new ball, then getting out to the back-up seamers or spinners in the twenties or thirties when batting should be getting easier. I thought it was a matter of concentration. I had a chat with him and told him that the first twenty runs of an innings were the most difficult. Once that was behind him, the rest should be easier – but that did not mean he could let his concentration slip. Every team he would play against in Pakistan would have quality spinners. He needed to develop a mindset that he was better than they were and they were not going to get him out. Then he would go on to seventies, eighties and hundreds. It was not rocket science, indeed it was sound batting common sense which I had developed in a playing career of a quarter of a century.

I was pleased to be able to pass on the benefit of that experience to someone half my age. He was an intelligent young man and prepared to listen. It worked. Five years later he was playing for Pakistan. He went on to play forty-seven Tests and with an average of 35.28 was an outstanding and reliable opening batsman throughout the 1990s.

Aamer was a slow left-arm bowler too, so perhaps I saw something of myself in him. He bowled outstandingly well against Habib Bank to achieve a personal best of four for 118, then bettered that in the second with seven for 35. It left us a victory target of 165 which we just reached with one wicket remaining, having been at one stage 151 for 2 before losing seven wickets for six runs. Against the Muslim Commercial Bank, Aamer had a hundred and I was delighted to be able to accompany him in a partnership of 88 for the third wicket.

I did not, however, see out the season with Lahore City as I was called up to join the Pakistan team touring India. On 21 February 1987, after a gap of 17 years and 111 days since my previous Test match – the third-longest in the history of the game – I was selected to play for my country. I had my old Glamorgan buddy Javed Miandad to thank. He had suggested to Imran Khan that, as a good player of spin bowling, I might be the answer to counter-act the Indian spin bowlers.

The two above me in the list with a longer interval between Test appearances are John Traicos, with over twenty-two years, and George Gunn, with almost eighteen. Traicos, who played for South Africa in 1970 and then for Zimbabwe in 1993, had no opportunity to play Test cricket because of South Africa's isolation from the international scene. Part of George Gunn's period of isolation between 1912 and 1930 was covered by the First World War. There were 104 Test matches that I missed out on, more than the other two missed during their absences, so it could be argued that mine was the longest period that a player has been isolated while continuously available for selection.

The third Test at Jaipur in which I made my comeback – the first time Jaipur had been used for a Test match – was marked by incident and controversy from the first ball when Sunil Gavaskar's new ultra-light pads caused his downfall, the ball ricocheting from an inside edge to third slip. It was a good batting pitch of which India made full use, taking their innings into a fourth day after the third had been washed out completely. We arrived on the third day to find sawdust patches on the pitch and concluded that there had been an attempt to change its condition. The Indian authorities contended that it had blown there from the outfield. Imran may well have put in an official protest, but the previous day the match had been visited by Pakistan's President, General Zia-ul-Haq, as part of his 'Cricket for Peace' mission and a protest would be seen in contradiction to that. We replied to India's 465 for 8 declared with 341, Rameez Raja's century avoiding the follow on. India's only hope of victory was gone.

The tension led to an onfield spat between Sunil Gavaskar and me. It was before the days of neutral umpires and the folklore is that Sunil was never given out lbw in India. I am not sure whether that is true or not, but in the second innings we were certainly convinced that we had him out on three or four occasions. It was handbags at dawn, the kind of thing that happens all over the world at all levels, nothing out of the ordinary. No one thought much of it and the after match handshakes and pleasantries were absolutely normal.

Indian and Pakistani cricketers have always got on well together. The rest day in the final Test at Bangalore coincided with the Hindu festival of Holi, a festival of colours which marks the beginning of spring. The hotel was festooned with blues, yellows, reds and greens and the players had great fun with coloured powders. No part of the hotel escaped the celebrations and the swimming pool and the public rooms underwent a transformation that must have been a nightmare for the cleaning staff. All the Pakistan players joined in, except Imran, who at first was a bit reluctant to participate. But we got him out later and threw him in the pool. He was not the only one to suffer that indignity. It was a fantastic day all round.

In between the third and fourth Test match, we had a relatively relaxed fixture in New Delhi against the Ranji Trophy champions, where I had my forty-sixth and final first-class century. The fourth Test at Ahmedabad ended in stalemate, the eleventh consecutive draw between the two countries. Sunil Gavaskar continued his glittering career by scoring his 10,000th Test run. On the fourth day when the Pakistan outfielders were pelted with stones and other missiles, Imran took the team off. When play resumed after fifty minutes, the tension was diffused as the team came out wearing helmets.

It was the last of my 460 first-class matches. If it seemed a long time since I made my debut as a schoolboy of fourteen, then it was – a few days under twenty-five years. When the team for the fifth and final Test was announced, I was dropped in favour of Javed, who had missed the fourth Test through injury.

In his autobiography, Javed Miandad maintains that my omission from the Bangalore Test was on account of my behaviour during the Ahmedabad Test. I complained of back trouble, was told to rest, but visited a nightclub. A feature on Cricket Web tells much the same story, but says it was a sore neck, that it was after the Test and that Imran was so furious that there was no way I would play for Pakistan again on his watch. There is no truth in either story. At no stage on that tour was I ever unfit – with a back injury, neck injury or any other sort of injury. Nightlife in Ahmedabad is not on the same scale as Delhi, Mumbai, Kolkata or Goya where there is a tourist market. There are few opportunities in what must rank as one of the most conservative cities in India. In any case, I was almost forty years old. Why, at that age, would I be visiting nightclubs? I can only surmise that the story arises from one questionable source and has developed into a malicious rumour which some accept as fact.

Perhaps the clearest defence against allegations that I had angered the management is that, ten days later, I was opening the batting in the third one-day international (and first since the Bangalore Test) in Hyderabad. True, I was not selected for the final Test in Bangalore, but my omission was more to do with the fact that Javed was available than to any disciplinary measures. If it were in Imran's mind that I should not be selected for those reasons, he did not consider the matter to be of such importance as to be mentioned in his autobiography.

Leaving aside my omission, in an attempt to end the seemingly interminable sequence of draws – now eleven on the trot – a turning, result pitch was prepared. Pakistan won a low scoring match by sixteen runs and took the Test series 1-0, but it was enough to satisfy the cricket-mad nation against the country from which it split in 1947.

Although it was great to win that Test match, I have to say that the Pakistan selection looked rather odd. It was obvious that the vast majority of the bowling would be undertaken by the spinners and so it turned out. So the selection of Saleem Jaffer as the third seamer was difficult to justify. He went in at number eleven, so clearly was not there for his batting, and did not bowl a single over in the match.

The Test series punctuated a one-day international series which we won 5-1. We had won the second ODI at Eden Gardens in Calcutta with three balls to spare, making hard work of chasing a total of 238 in forty overs, of which Krishna Srikkanth had 123. Higher totals are the norm now when forty or fifty-over cricket has become an extension of Twenty20 and judicious singles are replaced by continual attempts to clear the ropes. But at the time, a scoring rate of six an over was a big ask. Despite it being my first one-day international, I still had more experience of the game as a whole than most of my colleagues. As we left the field I suggested to Javed that rather than being stuck in the middle order and needing to score at nine or ten an over, it might be a better plan for me to open the innings with Rameez Raja to give me time to get a reasonable score and lay the foundations for later batsmen to accelerate. I was not without experience of opening the batting in limited overs matches, having done so for Surrey, Worcestershire and Glamorgan, although admittedly never in front of a crowd of 80,000. The plan would have the additional advantage of having a right hand/left hand combination at the top of the order. Javed put the proposal to captain Imran Khan, who agreed.

Brian Close had taught me the value of self-belief. His words of sixteen years earlier were ringing in my ears: Younis, there is no such thing as a superior bowler, no such thing as a superior batsman. If you are selected in the eleven, you are as good as anybody. It is not true, of course! Some batsmen and some bowlers are self-evidently better than others, but it is a great motivation. There is also a strong belief among Pakistani cricketers that they are capable of winning a match on their own. It is perhaps the opposite of team bonding which is so much in vogue these days, but it works more often than not. Wasim Akram and Waqar Younis certainly had such self-belief, as did Imran Khan. John Barclay, who captained Sussex, will relate tales of Imran saying 'captain, give me the ball' and producing a match-winning spell. My confidence on my one-day international debut was similar. Let *The Times* take up the story:

'Pakistan's openers, Rameez and Younis provided a solid start, putting on 106 before Rameez was held at long-off by Maninde off Shastri for 58 in the 22nd over.

With Miandad's dismissal soon after, Pakistan's chances seemed to fade as Shastri, the left arm spinner sent back Younis off his own bowling for 58 and Qadir and Manzoor for 9 and 14 respectively. Younis, aged thirty-nine, playing for Pakistan after an absence of seventeen years displayed considerable skill and stamina in his one-day international debut and delighted the 80,000 crowd with his exquisite driving and cutting.

With Pakistan struggling at 161 for five, Salim Malik entered the scene with only 7.3 overs left and 78 runs to get. But Malik showed no signs of anxiety, smashing 35 off the thirty-fifth and thirty-sixth overs and moving to 46 off twenty-one balls. Another thirteen off Madan Lal reduced the target to twelve for victory in the last over which was deservedly achieved with three balls to spare, Salim Malik fittingly obtaining the winning run with a crashing four past point off Kapil Dev.'

The one-day series should have been 6-0 had not the third match, at Hyderabad, been lost on a technicality. It was chaos at the end. As in the previous match, I opened with Rameez Raja, but was less successful this time, using my feet and getting stumped for 26. Two runs were required for a win from the last ball, both sides having lost six wickets. Abdul Qadir, a world-class bowler but far from a world-class batsman and on this occasion far from the most intelligent, took a run, but was run out going for a suicidal second. That gave India the match because they had now lost fewer wickets. Had he settled for the single, Pakistan would have won by virtue of being ahead at the 25-over mark. All this was explained to him before he went in, but in the heat of the moment, it clearly escaped his mind. An additional complication was that the last ball should have been called a no ball, the umpires failing to notice that there were only three fielders in the circle. Imran was furious with Abdul Qadir. He knew what was required. Why throw the game away?

For Pakistan to beat India, especially away, is a cause for great rejoicing and lifts the national mood. We had done so in both the Test and one-day international series. We were met at Lahore airport by a delirious crowd of around 60,000 people. We could scarcely believe it when we looked from the windows of the plane as we approached and saw the crowds and the police trying to control them. Celebrations went on for the next three days. We had a reception at Government House with President Zia-ul-Haq, receiving gold medals and 40,000 rupees each from the government by way of reward, a positive example this time of how politics and sport in Pakistan are interconnected. Allowing for inflation during the intervening period, the purse would today be equivalent to around ten times that, converting to something around £2,500 per player today. That bonus compared very well with the fee for my first Test match seventeen years earlier, which was insufficient to meet incidental expenses.

I was keen for more, but it represented my last taste of international and first-class cricket. I was assured by Imran that I was a strong candidate for the tour of England in 1989. My Test average had been good and compared with anything on this tour. I had finished third in the Test averages in that series with 44, behind Imran and Javed, slightly ahead of Rameez Raja and some way above everyone else. It also compared favourably with the previous tour of India by Pakistan ten years before. On the 1979/80 tour only two players had averaged above 30, but most survived to fight another day.

However, my name did not appear on the list when the squad for England was announced twelve days later. Not for the first time in my cricket career, I was extremely disappointed. On previous occasions I had contributed to the decision to leave me out of Pakistan squads, by electing to honour my contract with South Australia for 1972/73 and by going to South Africa in 1973/74. This time there were no administrative reasons not to select me. Yes, it could be argued that I was not good enough, but after recent seasons in England, that would not be an easy case to maintain. I thought I had a good chance, particularly after Imran's assurance. I thought I had a good, open and frank relationship with Imran, but I had no explanation from him or anyone else and I have not heard from him since.

I thought I had a role to play as elder statesman and advisor to the younger players. If you've not been before, England is not the easiest place to tour. There were a few county matches before the Test matches and more opportunity to acclimatise than there is now, and I felt I could help the youngsters, particularly the left handers, as well as make contribution in the middle order. Sure, I was thirty-nine, but I had looked after myself and stayed extremely fit. Misbah-ul-Haq was later to captain the side and score centuries at a similar age, going on well past his fortieth birthday.

My knowledge and expertise were available but apparently not required.

Cricket was given a grand reception in Dubai.

12

New Beginnings

Although cricket had been played in Kuwait since 1946, mainly by oil company expatriates, it was not until 1998 that the country became an affiliate member of the ICC. Inbetween there were spasmodic tours there under the leadership of Tom Graveney, Norman Gifford and an Air India XI, but it was from 1980 that it began to develop. That was the year I organised a benefit match there, a precedent followed by a number of players from the sub-continent, who do not have the advantages that English cricketers have, and subsequently cashed in.

My main involvement with cricket in the Middle East was, however, in Dubai. I was responsible for the introduction of the game there, a very ambitious project at the time. Now, along with Sharjah and Abu Dhabi, it is a major centre for international cricket and is home to the International Cricket Council. The oil industry had attracted ex-patriates from all over – England, India, Paki-

stan, Sri Lanka and Bangladesh – and such was their combined enthusiasm that a lot of league cricket was played
there. There were some high-class players. Some of them
had played in the Ranji Trophy, the first-class competition
in India; Abdul Qadir had played there and the standard
of cricket was quite good. When measured in flying time,
it was just round the corner from Pakistan, being about
an hour and a half from Karachi or Lahore.

The discovery of oil and its exploitation in the 1960s
saw Dubai develop into a global city and the business hub
of the Middle East. I was approached by the office of the
Emir of Dubai, Sheikh Rashid Al Maktoum, who saw the
potential to expand the game into the international area.
Would I be interested in organising that? I would! I began
work with a management consultant, Oscar Mandody,
who was on the personal staff of the Emir. It was a marketing opportunity not to be missed. Asked my advice,
I said that if he wanted to bring international players to
the Middle East, the best time would be late March and
early April between the southern hemisphere and northern hemisphere summers. Money was no object. The oil
was flowing.

Mr Mandody introduced me to the owner of the Al
Nasr stadium and football club, His Excellency Sheikh
Mana bin Khalifa al Maktoum, nephew of the Emir.
Football is very popular with the Arabs, cricket less so.
The club was managed by Don Revie, manager of the suc-
cessful Leeds United football team of the 1960s and early
1970s and subsequently of England and the UAE. Sheikh
Mana was a sports enthusiast and spent money on it from
a seemingly bottomless purse.

Like Kuwait the previous year, Dubai provided me with the opportunity for a couple of forty-over benefit matches which provided some compensation for what I had missed at Surrey. The Al Nasr stadium was at the time the only one in Dubai with floodlights, so was the obvious venue. This was in the days before the Dubai Sports City Stadium, opened in 2009, so cricket in Dubai began on a rubber mat on artificial turf spread across the centre circle of a football pitch.

The venture attracted world-class players and personalities from outside the game, including Sheikh Mana and Don Revie. In January 1981 the *Gulf News* gave a good write up to the proposals:

'It will be a benefit for Younis Ahmed, a world-class cricketer, born in Pakistan and blossomed in England.

Sir Garfield Sobers, considered to be the greatest cricketer of all times, will be in Dubai along with twenty-three other renowned players from all over the world to figure in two 40-over matches fixed for March 5 and 6.

Introducing Younis Ahmed at a Press conference at Dubai International hotel, Don Revie said Al Nasr [the UAE football team which he managed] would offer the best of support to this distinguished athlete in recognition of his dedicated fifteen-year service to the game of cricket.

He said Younis had met Sheikh Mana and "we are looking forward to a rare assemblage of the world's leading cricketers under the floodlights of Al Maktoum Stadium".

Pat Wright, Don Revie's Deputy, recalled that memorable innings of Younis he was privileged to watch last year. The place was Worcester, Pat's home county.

The morning was bright and pleasant. In the middle was this superb professional, producing strokes with a beautiful flow of action to all parts of the ground. Yorkshire attack was reduced to nothingness as Younis raced to a pre-lunch century.

Pat Wright's description was so vivid and lucid that one was driven back to that glorious morning.

Younis, his face radiating a smile, nodded his head in gratitude, and so did Saeed Ahmed, another of the finest one-down batsmen of his time, lending full assistance to his younger brother in his new role as promoter. He will also be playing in the matches.

Younis who is in Dubai for over a month narrated his exciting experience in this part of the world and thanked Sheikh Mana for becoming the Patron-in-Chief of the Dubai International World Cricket and Ricoh Watch people, Dubai International Hotel and Mr V Chanai for their sponsorship. Younis was flooded with questions from English as well as Arab press and he answered them with consummate ease. He however would not talk about his past, the bitter part of it.

The occasion was to portray the cricketing future of Dubai, nay the Gulf, and he did not like to digress. Abdullah Ibrahim, an official of the Youth and Sports Department and an ardent supporter of Al Nasr, who raised the curtain over the press conference, was equally fluent in translating Arabic into English.

Younis said his plan was to have big-time cricket in Dubai every year and considering the encouraging response he has received from Sheikh Mana, Don Revie, Pat

Wright, Abdullah Ibrahim and others, he was confident that he would "Inshallah" succeed in his mission

Younis said there would be two matches of 40-overs each, the first one on March 5 between England and a Pakistan-India combination. A rubber strip, the kind of which is used in England for indoor practice, would be fixed over the astroturf of the Al Nasr Club, one of the best in the world.

In the second match, Sobers and Rohan Kanhai will join England against an India-Pakistan selection.

The ball, he said, tended to skid on the artificial surface. With Imran Khan, the world's second-fastest bowler, in one of the line-ups, one could be assured of an exciting battle between the bat and the ball. "The wicket will be much more sporting than the ones Pakistan prepared for the series against the West Indies."

The play will start at 4pm and stretch through the night and make it a rare cricket show on earth, said Younis, adding that tickets would be placed on sale at all important places well on time for the convenience of thousands of cricket fans.'

Pat's memory lacks a little in accuracy. Yes, the century was against Yorkshire, but in the second innings of a Benson and Hedges match, so it could not have been before lunch, but poetic licence is permitted ahead of pedantry on this occasion.

I captained the India-Pakistan side, Tony Greig the other one. A star-studded side turned out in a significant and successful pioneering venture. The hospitality was outstanding, alcohol included, not a problem for overseas guests if served in five-star hotels, but otherwise generally prohibited in the UAE. The locals were delighted to meet cricketers and ask questions about the careers and experiences of Keith Fletcher, Graham Roope, Imran Khan, Zaheer Abbas and my brother Saeed. Tony Greig was a centre of attraction and loved the whole experience.

It was an all-round success and I was asked to stage similar matches the following year. Progress was rapid from there. The purpose-built Dubai Cricket Stadium replaced cricket on a rubber mat, as well as providing an athletics track and facilities for football, basketball and Australian Rules football. Sharjah and Abu Dhabi both had cricket facilities and soon all three became centres for regular international cricket, later providing an ideal opportunity for Pakistan to play 'home' matches which could not be staged in its own cricket centres. The UAE also hosts international tournaments in its own right, provides an opportunity for pre-season warm weather training and practice matches for English counties as well as hosting the MCC v Champion County match.

The only downside is that Pakistan's Test matches in the Middle East attract few spectators. The age and employment profile is different from other parts of the world. County cricket in England is watched mainly by the older, retired generation, but that clientele does not feature in the UAE. Almost all are working during the week. There is a bit of a spike in the attendance graph for Thursdays and Fridays, the Middle East weekend; and limited over matches, especially Twenty20, attract larger gates. Additionally, the Dubai ground is away from the city centre and public transport facilities are inadequate, but those are likely to improve and form part of an infrastructure built on finance generated by oil which is likely to continue as long as that substance is indispensible to world trade.

One of my honoured guests at the benefit match in Dubai was the well-known Bollywood actor, Dilip Kumar, with his wife, Saira Banu. He is a legend, admired in both India and Pakistan, a successful actor and producer whose career in the film industry dominated six decades and included over sixty films. Dilip Kumar is his stage name. His real name is Yousaf Khan, but to me, he will always be Yousaf Bhai (a term of affection – literally 'brother' in Hindi) and his wife will always be Saira Bhabhi (sister-in-law). I had stayed with them at their house in the Pali Hill district of Mumbai. In seven of his films, including his own production of Gunga Jamuna, he starred with Vyjayanthamila, a great and beautiful actress, Bollywood's Ava Gardner. He co-starred with a number of other beautiful women, including Mathu Bala, Meena Qumari and Nargis. All set the rumour mills grinding full time, but in the end he met and married Saira. Both were very popular additions to the cricket personalities in the UAE. The public loved them and both had a fabulous time in Dubai.

They were not the only Bollywood stars who I could count among my friends. Despite the political differences, I always enjoyed visiting India and was friendly with Farokh Engineer, Bishen Bedi, Ashok Mankad and former captain, Ajit Wadekar. It was through them I got to know some Bollywood stars and developed strong friendships.

Another good friend was the late Yash Chopra, director and producer, who was originally from Lahore before
partition. Whenever Yash was in London we would dine
together in the fashionable Beauchamp Place, off Knightsbridge, where he always asked me to book a table. He was
one of the most humble and honest people I have met.
He gave me so much wisdom about life. I shall always be
grateful to him.

I will never forget the occasion when he invited me to
a film set to watch superstar Amitabh Bachchan (Big B
as he was popularly known) and the great and beautiful
actress Rekha recording a scene for the film *Silsila*. It was
a short scene, shot in the Marriott Hotel, Delhi. When
it was completed, we adjourned to the hotel restaurant.
Amitabh was unfortunately suffering from a bad cold and
unable to join us, but it was a great pleasure and privilege
to dine with Rekha, Yash Chopra and his friends. I did
meet Amitabh Bachchan on other occasions. He was a
man whose philosophy of life I very much admired. He
was not enamoured of the Indian caste and class system.

All the actors and actresses I met knew their cricket
and were keen to talk about it, always enquiring about
my international comeback after seventeen years. They
wanted to know what it was like to play at Eden Gardens
in Calcutta, in front of 80,000 people, wondering what it
would be like in their own profession if they were suddenly thrust in front of a camera after seventeen years away.
I explained it was not as difficult as that. I had continued
to play the game in between and there were times when
county cricket in England was tougher than Test cricket
and overseas tours.

They were fascinated by my descriptions of the changing atmospheric conditions in England, where there could be three different kinds of weather in one day, and the difficulty of scoring runs there. They had no concept of professional cricketers playing every day and doing it for a living. They wanted to know how good were Garry Sobers, Vivian Richards, Saeed Ahmed; how quick were Lillee, Thompson, Holding, Sylvester Clarke and Imran Khan, how great was Hanif Mohammed. Likewise, I was interested in knowing about their films! We had some long and fascinating conversations. I loved every minute of it.

There is now a strong connection between Bollywood and the Indian Premier League. They are both about entertainment, both highly successful and to an extent feed off each other. Financially too, there are links, some of the teams being owned by Bollywood superstars. Shahrukh Khan owns the Kolkata Knight Riders and Shilpa Shetty and her husband, Raj Kundra, own the Rajasthan Royals, while Preity Zinta has a share in the ownership of Kings XI Punjab. Businessman Mukesh Ambani, chairman of Reliance Industries whose personal wealth is estimated to be in excess of US $20 billion, finances Bollywood parties and owns the Mumbai Indians. So there is money around – and plenty of it. When Bollywood and cricket meet – as they did in those early years of cricket in the UAE – good things can happen.

From cricketer to restaurateur . . . Younis Ahmed and wife Puchi in their Johannesburg eaterie

Puchi and I at Shezan,
the first Pakistani restaurant in Johannesburg.

13

Food For Thought

I have always had an interest in and passion for food. As a professional cricketer, whether batting or fielding, I never thought it sensible to eat much during the day, but I made up for it in the evenings. I enjoyed eating out, enjoying Chinese food especially, but also Italian, Portuguese and of course, Pakistani cuisine. So, when it came to looking for business opportunities outside the game, a restaurant seemed to be the obvious answer.

In 1980, I bought a restaurant in Hampstead, a few minutes walk from the underground station, an upmarket area of the capital. As it turned out, the restaurant was very close to the residence of a famous actor, Peter O'Toole, himself a cricket enthusiast and a very pleasant man who became a regular customer. There were a number of actors and artists – and millionaires – in the area, so it was going to be a tremendous challenge. George Michael and Queen were among our customers. I had always enjoyed eating out, but now I was on the other side of the fence, no longer soaking in customer satisfaction, but providing it.

Cooking is both an art and a challenge to the chefs when orders from four or five tables come in, perhaps simultaneously, and all have to be on the table within fifteen minutes – about the time a customer would expect to wait. Half an hour or forty minutes would be too long. It was a different world from professional sport. I was still involved heavily in cricket, so was very dependent on Puchi to keep the business running. Her expertise in catering was a tremendous help. Puchi, although a tremendous cook, did very little in the way of actual cooking. Her role was rather to oversee the quality of the food and service.

We had a manager, three chefs and about fourteen other staff. It became a very popular venue. To give it a cricket theme, I called it The Bombay Pavilion. It was a profitable business, particularly at weekends, thanks to quality food, good service and good manners. Poor and clumsy service, long waits for cold, semi-cold or tasteless food does not encourage repeat business, so we managed to succeed in avoiding those pitfalls.

Working late and driving back from Hampstead to Epsom in the small hours of the morning takes its toll, both mentally and physically. We eliminated the commuting time after one year of operation by moving in above the shop, converting the space above the restaurant to two flats, one for ourselves and one for the manager. Even with reduced travelling, however, there was no time for birthday parties, weddings and sporting events. One's own social life had to be put on hold and leisure time was generally non-existent. Nevertheless, we made some fabulous friends while we were in Hampstead.

We continued that first business until 1988, during which time I combined being restaurateur with playing cricket for Worcestershire and Glamorgan, in Australia and for Pakistan. By the time I hung up my cricket gear, we thought it time to move on. Parking in that part of Hampstead is never easy and we lost income because potential customers were unable to stop and moved on and found somewhere else.

We were reminded of the three essentials: location, location and location.

Now that I was no longer playing first-class cricket, we could look further afield. We saw a similar opportunity in the affluent northern suburbs of Johannesburg, a city which had no Pakistani or Indian restaurants. In the apartheid era that was not an issue as the Group Areas Act had kept the ethnic groups separate, but a more open society with more freedom of movement meant that there was now a gap in the market for such a venture. We opened up our new restaurant – the Shezan – in Norwood in 1993.

I was busy with my coaching academies in Johannesburg and Durban, so once again Puchi took the reins and ran the restaurant. Three chefs were flown in from Pakistan and the Pakistan cricket team were at the time making their first tour to South Africa, so that was a good time for meeting old friends, Javed Miandad and Wasim Akram in particular, and doing a bit of business as well.

Partly because of its location and partly because of my reputation as a cricketer from some twenty years earlier, the Shezan became a celebrity venue. Opposition leader

Tony Leon was a regular customer and loved Shezan's food. The press picked up the story and we had several favourable write ups in newspapers and glossy magazines. We were privileged to entertain cricketers, rugby players, cabinet ministers and a number of golfers, both local and international, of whom Gary Player, a massive celebrity in South Africa, was the best known. Louis Luyt, President of the South African Rugby Football Union, was also a guest. At six feet six inches, he was an imposing presence at any gathering. As a result of knowing Louis, Puchi and I were invited to the President's Box at the 1995 World Cup Final at Ellis Park – a fantastic experience. Past South African rugby stars, President Mandela and government ministers all joined in the celebrations as South Africa beat New Zealand. Most of the spectators stayed in the packed stadium long after the final whistle and presentations. For anyone there it was an experience they will never forget.

Norwood borders Houghton, where Nelson Mandela had his residence. He was among our more distinguished guests, his favourite dish being chicken burani. But I first met President Mandela at the Wanderers on the first day of the South Africa-India Test Match in 1992, when I was honoured to be a guest in the President's box. We were all introduced to him, but of course there were so many guests, we had only about thirty seconds each. During that time I found him utterly charming and statesman-like. He looked straight into my eyes and had a very firm handshake and said, 'Good to meet you.' It was one of the most electrifying experiences of my life. I can understand why so many people, including world leaders, have found him so charismatic.

However, although we made money from the Shezan, like the earlier restaurant in Hampstead, it became too time-consuming in the end. The restaurant industry is a tough business, sacrifices have to be made and it is not something that can continue indefinitely. We decided to call it a day, relax and enjoy ourselves a bit. It had, however, been an invaluable business and lifestyle experience, helping me to get to grips with the real world which exists outside the bubble of professional cricket.

Toasting success with Jonty Rhodes
at the Younis Ahmed Cricket Academy.

14

Investing in the Future

'Coaching is for kids and for telling players when to get their hair cut,' said Brian Clough, and it is true that there is less need for coaching at the professional levels of sport where the job is more likely to involve honing existing techniques and leaving players to work out for themselves what works for them, perhaps concentrating on the psychology of the game and, for captains, man management. However, at grassroots level, there is a case for good coaching so that sound cricketing habits can be drilled into young players. That is not to say that every player should come out the same. What a boring game it would be if that were the case!

Coaching is an art based on science. I have seen many young cricketers without talent and sometimes without interest – in those cases one perhaps has to limit oneself to the basics – line and length and playing straight. But where there is something there, the coach's job is to develop that gift so that mediocre players become good ones and good ones become very good ones.

I was lucky enough to be well coached as a youngster and will always have a debt of gratitude to men like Agha Saadat Ali, Nazar Mohammad and Maqsood Ahmed who, at school and club level, set me on the road to professional cricket. Later, at Surrey, Arthur McIntyre kept me on the rails. I obtained my own coaching qualifications in Melbourne in 1983 under the tutelage of Frank Tyson, who was Director of the Coaching Academy for the State of Victoria, so that during and after my playing career I have been able to give something back to the game I love. Coaching has changed almost beyond recognition since my early days when there would be instruction and discussion on stance, grip and movement towards the ball. Now it's all about workouts in the gym, building up shoulders and forearms to whack the ball over the ropes.

My first coaching experience was in what was then Rhodesia, tacked on to my Derrick Robins tours in South Africa. In post-apartheid days, I managed a coaching academy in Johannesburg, hiring coaches and supplementing local men by flying in distinguished former West Indian players Phil Simmons and Alvin Kallacharan. Jonty Rhodes also made an invaluable contribution and Graeme Pollock made the occasional guest appearance. The boys certainly benefited from their vast expertise. The academy also ran for a year in Durban, but the distance made the logistics difficult and I had to discontinue that. There were, black, white and Indian children – continuing the quest to break down the colour bar that I first began when touring South Africa in 1973 – and I am proud to be able to look back on it as a successful venture.

My aim was to produce players good enough to represent provincial sides and the national team in the new South Africa. After apartheid had gone as a political institution, the social effects remained. White cricketers were always likely to be better than non-white ones because they were able to enjoy vastly superior facilities and there was inevitably going to be a time lag before they reached the same standard. Quota systems were introduced with a number of places, perhaps four, reserved for black, coloured and Asian players. While this method might have given those players opportunities they would not otherwise have had, the downside was that good, sometimes very good, white players saw their chances thwarted by players who, in cricketing terms, were their inferiors. Hence Kevin Pietersen and others were lost to South African cricket. It was not the answer. It would be far better to work at bringing non-white players up to standard to provide high class multi-racial cricket. A good standard of league cricket was essential. Youngsters will learn far more playing a tough high-standard game than any number of hours in the nets. There is no alternative.

Later, I coached at Gresham's School in Norfolk for the 2005 and 2006 seasons. The school, situated in Holt, dates from 1555 and was the foundation of a wealthy landowner and philanthropist, Sir John Gresham. MCC have an annual fixture there. The Headmaster, Anthony Clark, informed me that the school already had a very successful coach in Alan Ponder, a Cambridge graduate, who had played Minor Counties cricket with Cambridgeshire.

He was an opening bat and wicketkeeper and a great socialiser. We got on tremendously well and Alan made my job very easy. He respected my cricketing knowledge and allowed me to coach the youngsters in my own way.

We played other schools on the circuit and I was able to meet and enjoy the company of other coaches like John Lever, Derek Randall, Raymond East, David Steele and my old Surrey colleague Geoff Howarth, all of whom I had played with and against – so it was a good standard of schools cricket. Felix Flower, Andrew Clark and Charlie Ponder were among my star players. Felix went on to play for Norwich, Norfolk, Cardiff University and also had a few matches with Glamorgan 2nd XI, but from a career point of view, the city was a more attractive option for him.

It was also a pleasure to meet General (now Lord) Richard Dannatt, Chief of the General Staff of the Army. His daughter was studying at Gresham and he was invited to play for the Headmaster's XI against Alan Ponder's XI. The younger Dannatt had no chance to don whites, however, because although it was a co-educational school, the girls did not play cricket. That is likely to change as women's cricket becomes more significant both nationally and internationally, particularly under such talented players and charismatic leaders as Charlotte Edwards. The enthusiasm is certainly there, so in many cases is the ability. What is lacking perhaps is physical strength (that's an anatomical thing and there's probably nothing to be done about it), tactical awareness and judgement of shot selection, like hitting to mid-off, mid-on and mid-wicket rather than playing straight. There is a huge coaching job to be done, but with more money in the game, we are on the way.

Later I did some coaching with Harpenden Cricket Club at the instigation of Chairman Geoff Newman. It was a good socialising club, but an entirely amateur one comprising weekend cricketers, many of whom commuted to London in the week and played cricket purely for fun. Geoff, along with Director of Cricket David Doyle, was looking for the club to become more professional in their attitude and was keen to improve their standard of play with a view to becoming one of the best clubs in Hertfordshire. They both worked tirelessly to that end and I was happy to help them and take the club forward. Harpenden had five teams, all in leagues, and there was scope for improvement at all levels. We managed to blend new faces and experienced players such as Nick Lamb, son of Tim, former Chief Executive of TCCB, and Ben Frazer. Both went on to on to play Minor Counties cricket with Hertfordshire. I like to think that I played a major role in improving 1st XI standards and attitudes. I loved the Hertfordshire countryside and the town itself and enjoyed the challenge during the six years I spent there. At the same time I was coaching at St Albans School where the Head Coach was Chris Hudson. I had a lot of time and respect for Chris – a very hardworking and knowledgeable sportsman.

I love coaching and it is a pleasure to watch the development of young (and, sometimes, not so young) cricketers. It is so important for former players to give something back to the game that gave so much to them.

Meeting the Don – with Sir Donald Bradman during
my time with South Australia.

15

Great Players of My Time

Many autobiographies contain a side of the best players the author has played with and against. I thought about doing that, but found it just too difficult. There would be only eleven places available and in my twenty-seven years in the game, I have come across so many that it would be invidious to make a selection. Furthermore, there would be no wicketkeeper and I would find it impossible to single out a captain from the several excellent ones I have played under. Misbah-ul-Haq I have excluded on the grounds that we are not really contemporary, but I believe he is the best captain Pakistan have had, ahead of Imran and of Javed. Although advancing in age, he remains fitter than some of the younger members of the squad. He took over in the wake of Salman Butt's inglorious departure and with Pakistan not being able to play in their own country (despite rare exceptions like the Zimbabwe one-day series in 2015) has welded the squad into a well-balanced and winning combination.

Nor have I been able to include Kevin Pietersen as I never had the pleasure of playing with or against him, but I have seen him play on several occasions and he has to go down as one of the greats of any era. I do not know what has gone on in the England dressing room and he can obviously be a tricky man to handle at times. But it seems to be almost criminal to ignore a talent like that and deprive the cricket-watching public of his special brand of entertainment. He was the backbone of England's batting line up and still had three or four years to offer. His treatment has been a disgrace to the game and he should still be playing international cricket. The other side of the argument is that he was not a good influence in the dressing room, a place where it is important to maintain harmony. But management – in cricket and in business – is about handling difficult characters. That's what managers get paid for. Good management includes dealing with them and getting the most out of their talents. There are a number of instances of the Pakistan Cricket Board failing to do that in the past and simply sidelining or banning players. It is sad to see the ECB following suit. Sport is full of strong characters, but part of a captain's job is to reconcile different personalities, different views and different approaches to the game and take to the field as one unit. Whatever views KP may have expressed in the dressing room, however much disliked he was by other players, however much he may have disliked them, as long as he was making runs, he should have been picked.

I also never played against Sir Donald Bradman, but there is no doubt in my mind that he was the greatest batsman of all time. When I first met him, it was difficult to appreciate that this modest and unassuming man with no airs and graces was one who had such a huge impact on the game and whose dominance was such that he was the cause of a novel and hostile means of attack. Statistics do not mean everything, but a Test average of 99.94 (more than 50% above the next highest) and a century every third occasion he went to the wicket are ones which are impossible to ignore.

Of the batsmen I have played with and against, Sunil Gavaskar will be remembered as one of the greatest of all time. He played no greater innings than his 221 against the odds at The Oval in 1979 when India almost succeeded in chasing down a target of 438. I first saw him bat and remember having a chat with him when he toured with the Indian team; I was at Worcester. He was less instinctive and more textbook than many of his compatriots. As an opening bat, he was ahead of his time, a genius of a player. He scored a number of hundreds in the West Indies, playing against that magnificent pace attack – Andy Roberts, Michael Holding, Malcolm Marshall, Joel Garner – no mean performers, any of them. It exploded once and for all the myth that Indian batsmen could not play pace bowling. It had been true once when Fred Trueman had helped reduce India to 0 for 4 at Headingley in 1952, but no more. Gavaskar's technique, lightness of footwork and concentration were amazing. He just loved batting and never seemed to get tired. The longer he batted, the more comfortable he looked and was equally at home against pace or spin, even on turning pitches. He was the first Indian to score 1,000 Test runs in a calendar year.

Sachin Tendulkar was a high-class player with a phenomenal record. He could play long innings and was capable of destroying any attack. He started very young and played for a long time, a prodigy who believed in showing the bowler the full face of the bat. We may have to wait some time before we see anyone else equal his remarkable achievement of a hundred centuries in international cricket.

Barry Richards was an extraordinarily talented player. I have come across no other batsman who saw the ball as early and got into position as quickly – and this from the first ball. He averaged 54.74 in first-class matches. Because 'balls faced' was not recorded in his early matches there is no accurate record of his strike-rate, but for an opening batsman it must have been exceptional. His bat looked about twice the width of the stumps. Sadly politics prevented what would surely have been a very successful Test career for South Africa.

Geoffrey Boycott was another opener I admired very much. He coped with the world's best in bowler-friendly conditions. He was also an outstanding player of spin bowling. An admirer of Sir Leonard Hutton and a deep thinker, he had the opening batsman's art of not only having all the strokes, but knowing when to use them.

Saeed Ahmed, my brother, batted at number three for Pakistan for most of his career. Whatever might be said or written about his volatile temperament or brushes with authority, there were few who could match his elegance, particularly that of his cover drive. I learned a lot from talking to him and watching him bat. He scored 1,000 runs in eleven Test matches, eight of them against a strong West Indies side.

I also learned from Glenn Turner, who dominated the Worcestershire scene when I was at New Road and had done so for several seasons before. Early in his career he had a reputation for being strokeless, but that was unjustified. He had all the strokes, but shot selection is a key part of batting. He could defend for long periods when required and it often was – New Zealand's batting was more fragile than it is now – but in the right circumstances, he could unleash the full range of his artillery, never more so than at New Road when he scored a triple century against Warwickshire, bringing up his hundredth century in the process.

Vivian Richards was perhaps the most eye-catching batsman I came up against. He never wore a helmet, even when they were part of the scene, relying on his incredible eye to deal with anything bowled at him. I have done a bit of coaching and sometimes wonder how a coach would have dealt with Viv. As far as I am aware he did not have any flaws and in any case, there is no way any coach could teach the skill of picking up a yorker on off stump and depositing it into the crowd behind square leg.

The best of the rest? Martin Crowe, Ted Dexter and Rohan Kanhai.

In terms of bowlers, Abdul Qadir was a master of his craft of leg spin, almost impossible to 'pick'. Also difficult to pick in a very different way and of a different craft was Dennis Lillee, who bowled with his brain as much as his body. Although no one enjoyed facing him, there was universal admiration for the beauty of his action and his bowling skills.

I grew up in a country where youngsters learned to bowl in hot and dry conditions and, because of the rough uneven grounds (or even streets) the ball is roughed up very quickly, encouraging the art of reverse swing. In normal swing bowling, the shine follows the outside of the curve, but in reverse swing, as the name suggests, the opposite is the case. The huge advantage of reverse swing is that it can be bowled at speed (say 85 mph), whereas in conventional swing, the choice is between swing and pace – the greater the pace, the less the swing and vice versa. Allegedly invented by Sarfraz Nawaz (though there are other claimants), reverse swing requires that one side of the ball must be kept dry and smooth, while the other must be kept rough – by whatever means. Before it became illegal under the 1980 revision of the Laws of Cricket, it was common practice for spin bowlers to rub the ball in the dirt to enable them to get a better grip; swing bowlers with an eye to reverse swing did the same. Since then, however, it has been less easy to roughen up one side of the ball. Fielding sides have resorted to bowling or throwing in a non-rotating ball with the rough side towards the ground or – more questionably, using buckles, bottle tops and finger nails.

Pakistan-reared players all learned to respond to the challenge of bowling a maximum of perhaps half a dozen overs in a spell, the heat preventing any more than that, and getting the ball to do something on slow, low, unhelpful, grassless pitches. Among them, Waqar Younis and Wasim Akram mastered the art of bowling not only quickly and accurately, but also of controlling the swing both ways. Imran Khan was Wasim's hero and mentor; Wasim a willing pupil who, with Waqar, continued the art of reverse swing into the 1990s. One right handed, one left, they formed one of the most devastating opening attacks in the history of the game, starting with conventional swing, then switching to reverse, as one side of the ball got rougher, the other being kept perfectly dry. Wasim had 414 wickets in 104 Test matches at 23.62, Waqar 373 wickets in 87 matches at 23.56.

Although I could never count Imran Khan as one of my friends and have had my differences with him, I cannot let that colour my judgment about his cricketing ability. He has no challengers to his status as the best all-rounder that Pakistan has produced. There have been great batsmen who bowled a bit and great bowlers who batted a bit, but at his peak, he could have been picked to play international cricket for either. He was also a deep-thinking captain as well as a great student of the game and always prepared to adjust his own game, such as amending his double-barrelled action to enable him to bowl reverse swing. He continued learning and became an outstanding exponent of the art of reverse swing bowled at speed. In eighty-eight Test matches he had 362 wickets at 22.81, an average not very different from his overall first-class figure. Imran could also bat a bit, averaging 37.69 in Test matches and slightly less in all first-class matches, underlining his own contention that he could produce the goods when it really mattered. Almost alone of Pakistan players in the late 1970s, he was considered good enough to play for Kerry Packer's World Series Cricket World XI and learned from the great players, particularly Dennis Lillee, he played with and against.

However, in Imran's judgment (and there would be very little dissent in the cricket world) there are no challengers to Garry Sobers' position as the greatest all-rounder the game has ever produced. He had the attribute, common to world-class batsmen, of seeing the ball early and playing it late, going on the back foot to a swinging ball, still middling it and playing attacking strokes. He could bat in any position in the order. As a bowler, he excelled in three different styles; orthodox slow left-arm, chinaman, or pace bowling as quick as anyone, including Holding, Marshall and Clarke. He also fielded well in any position, though slip was his specialism where he took some unbelievable catches.

Other all-rounders who played in my time were Richard Hadlee, Ian Botham and Kapil Dev; great players all of them and strong competition between them to be second to Garry – although Imran would get my vote.

A good cricket team requires a good leader on the field. I have probably said enough about Micky Stewart for readers to be aware of my admiration for him. He was a leader who knew his own mind, but was nevertheless prepared to listen and to help his junior players. He was also a distinguished footballer and later gained much respect in roles as Cricket Manager with both Surrey and England.

Brian Close was one of the toughest characters I have ever met, both mentally and physically. Unlike some captains – he could handle difficult characters and there were a few of them around in his England and Yorkshire teams! He had in his dressing room one Geoffrey Boycott, a role model for difficult characters. But, although strategies and tactics may be discussed in dressing rooms, matches are won or lost on the field of play. Whatever upsets he might have caused among those with whom he shared a dressing room, Boycott's name was inevitably the first on the team sheet. However, if Boycott then batted too slowly, Close would let him know: 'Boycs, you were 40 not out. The ball was old. We needed bonus points. You were more concerned with getting your century and you lost us two points.' Close's tactical and motivational skills have already been mentioned. It was a pleasure and an education to play under him.

Among other captains, Tony Greig stands out as a magnetic and charismatic leader. Not always the most diplomatic and frequently at daggers drawn with the establishment, he had an unerring belief in his own ability which he transferred to his players. He played an important part, being at the forefront of the Packer revolution.

Gaddafi Stadium in Lahore – hopefully international cricket will return to my home town soon.

16

Rising from the Mire

In Pakistan in 1947, hockey was dominant and cricket was a minority sport. Cricket was burdened by being seen as the game of the British Raj and the upper echelons of society. However, after partition and as the country settled into an uneasy independence, cricket spread to the masses and challenged hockey as the national sport. From being the preserve of the gymkhanas, colleges and schools, stimulated by the advent of televised matches which created a national publicity previously only possible through newspapers and radio, it spread to the masses. I remember people in crowds of perhaps five or six hundred listening to radio commentary inside and outside cafés.

Cricket was played on the streets and on waste ground, anywhere where there was space to accommodate it. The equipment was often rudimentary, bats were any piece of wood that could be found and balls were manufactured from melted down footballs or tape balls – tennis balls wrapped round with insulating tape. It spread even further and raised enthusiasm among women and later in Afghanistan. Under Abdul Hafeez Kardar and later under Imran Khan the game became better administered, although many fell by the wayside if they dared to challenge those influential but tyrannical characters. Cricket became intertwined with politics and the national team was a source of pride or scorn.

An adjective which has frequently been used of Pakistan and its cricketers is 'mercurial', and it has to be recognised that volatility, both in temperament and on the field performance, is very much part of the national psyche. Pakistan can snatch a win in a match which looks lost or they can be cruising to victory and then throw it away. In both cases questions are raised: whether such fluctuations are due to accident or design. It is often assumed, rightly or wrongly, that there has been an element of match fixing. I have never been approached by a bookmaker or anyone involved in the betting and gaming industry, but there is strong evidence that it does go on and it is reasonable to assume that those cases which have come to light are just the tip of a very murky iceberg.

Corruption and match fixing is not new and there are plenty of examples in English cricket in the two hundred years before Pakistan was created. Matches were played for huge purses and bets placed on the results. Bookmakers were prominent at Lord's during the nineteenth century. Human nature and greed being what it is, there was a temptation – frequently yielded to – for those bookmakers and gambling spectators to arrange the results of matches to line their own pockets and those of the players whose performances (or underperformances) contributed to the result. Pakistan did not invent match fixing and in recent years there have been investigations and court cases which have uncovered its existence elsewhere, but they are among the first to be mentioned when it is up for discussion.

There is a distinction between match fixing and spot fixing. To pre-determine the result of a match requires the whole team (or most of them) to be involved and, ideally, some complicity from the opposition as well. That takes a bit of organising. It takes only one whistleblower and everyone is in trouble. Much easier is spot fixing, where bets are placed on the number of runs scored or wickets taken in an over or block of overs – or, easier still to organise, in which over a wide or no ball will be bowled. That is what happened in the England-Pakistan Test at Lord's in 2010 when Mohammad Amir, under instructions from captain Salman Butt, deliberately bowled a very obvious no ball. I am sure there have been other examples in the game that have gone undetected and the players have got away with it. Not on this occasion, however. It was rumbled by a smart piece if investigative journalism from the *News of the World*.

Mohammad Amir was desperately unlucky to receive a five-year ban for the spot fixing scandal at Lord's. He is from a humble background and it was his first time away from home. He was understandably keen to impress his captain and would do anything to please him. Youngsters receive no advice on who to associate with and who to avoid and naturally follow the lead from their captain, in this case Salman Butt, the real villain of the piece. Given his age and inexperience, a stern reprimand for Amir might have been sufficient – a view shared by the majority of people to whom I have spoken in Australia, South Africa, England India and Pakistan in recent years.

Michael Atherton has been consistent in his support for Amir, writing about the case in *The Times* and interviewing him on television. He takes the view, as I think most of us would, that everyone deserves a second chance in life. It looks as though Amir has been given that. He has served his time in prison and the slate has been wiped clean. Mohammad Asif and Salman Butt are still undergoing rehabilitation and their re-integration is more uncertain. They are older and should have known better, especially Salman, who had responsibilities as captain which, at any level of the game, embraces far more than leading the team and taking charge on the field. There is a public relations side and a responsibility to the wider game and its spirit. On those he has failed, so it is right that his second chance should take longer in coming. It is right that all three should be given another opportunity, but also right that the timescale for each should be different.

On the other hand, Kevin Pietersen, Graeme Swann and others have taken the opposite view and said that the bans should be permanent. Some Pakistan players, taking the moral high ground, have said that they would be unwilling to share a dressing room with Amir if he is reinstated. They are perfectly entitled to that opinion, but it does seem hard on him. Someone of more mature years might have questioned those instructions or reported the matter to the appropriate authorities. But this was a youngster on his first tour. He deserves a bit of compassion.

Pakistan has had its fair share of publicity for cheating and match fixing, but they are far from being alone. There are other recorded instances in addition to the Lord's no-ball incident for which the three Pakistan players were punished. Danish Kaneria and Mervyn Westfield were found guilty of accepting bribes to concede an agreed number of runs in an over while playing for Essex. The Hansie Cronje case and the conviction of former India captain Mohammad Azharrudin (who has since, perhaps appropriately, turned his attention to politics) demonstrate that it is a worldwide issue.

In late 2015 Chris Cairns was acquitted at Southwark Crown Court, although some of the evidence pointed to a very murky hinterland in cricket. Unproven rumours abound, including those surrounding the Australia-Pakistan Test at Sydney in 2010. Pakistan, having led by over 200 on the first innings, capitulated in the second to lose by 36 runs.

However, of thirty players listed in the 2015 edition of *Wisden* banned after being found guilty of or admitting fixing cricket, only seven are from Pakistan. It is no defence that everyone else is doing it, but it needs to be recognised as a worldwide issue.

Match fixing is a cancer in the game that has to be rooted out. The paying public deserve better. When they part with their hard-earned cash to watch a sporting contest, they expect to see a fair competition with each side striving to win. But there are a number of low key one-day series around the world and there are also dead rubbers.

Where the result does not matter, where a bribe to lose a match exceeds by many times the win bonus and there is little chance of getting caught, a player might think: why not? The disparity between the pay of top players and run-of-the-mill players, who might not be certain of regular selection, make the possibility of easy money for doing not very much particularly tempting. What to do about it?

The answer from the authorities' point of view is to encourage teams to play within the spirit of cricket, but that is a bit woolly. Words are cheap and have to be backed up by action, which involves increasing the chances of getting caught. The ICC's Anti-Corruption Unit has gone far in banning mobile phones and other devices capable of outside contact from players' areas.

But perhaps more is needed. International cricket is well policed, but it is only the tip of a huge iceberg and, when matches below that level are broadcast live overseas, there is no way that the whole world of cricket can be policed. Maybe it is a question of changing attitudes so any thought of fixing becomes taboo.

Part of the difficulty is that betting in India and Pakistan is illegal. It goes on, of course, and everybody knows that, but because it is underground, it is virtually impossible to monitor. My protégé, Aamir Sohail, has suggested that if the industry were legalised (although not all bookmakers would wish to be part of such a set up) some would welcome the opportunity to operate above board and it would be easier to identify irregular betting patterns and target sources of the corruption.

The prominence of Indian bookmakers, however illegal their operations, means that there will always be a threat to cricket. The knowledge of what has gone before and the threat of a spell behind bars should be deterrent enough, but I suppose that if players think the odds of getting away with spot or match fixing are in their favour and the bribe exceeds, often by many times, the prize money for winning a match, then there is always going to be the temptation, particularly perhaps for those coming to the end of their career or those who have a pretty good idea that they are not going to make it anyway. It is far from a comfortable issue. Education is paramount and the ICC must continue to be vigilant. But it is not only the ICC. Every cricket board must have a system, covering all the clubs, who should be made aware of the dangers. The public, however partisan, wish to see a fair contest between two teams on the field of play, not one where the outcome has already been decided in the back streets of Mumbai. We all have an obligation to observe the spirit of cricket and that obligation embraces saying no to match fixing.

A commission under the chairmanship of Justice Malik Qayyum, which reported in 1999, produced some fairly damning conclusions, naming and shaming leading Pakistan players and recommending fines. The enquiry ran concurrently with the investigation of rather more serious corruption charges against Benazir Bhutto and her husband Asif Ali Zardari. However, not much happened as the presentation of the report coincided with the fall of Nawaz Sharif's government. The new President, General Musharraf, who was also patron of Pakistan Cricket, was anxious to smooth things over. However, the report had highlighted a strain of corruption which reflected no credit on some of the country's top players. Although it was only partially implemented, perhaps we can hope that its memory and the publicity attending the convictions of the three Lord's culprits will encourage players to believe that match and spot fixing are not only not worth it, but also morally wrong. We will soon witness its reduction and maybe its elimination. Or is that being too optimistic?

The other aspect of the game for which Pakistan has become notorious, though again not the only offenders, has been in what the Laws of Cricket refer to as 'changing the condition of the ball'. Cricket, perhaps more than any other game, is dependent on the condition of the ball. What is legal and what is not is complex and has varied over time, but basically the fielding side may polish and dry the ball and remove mud, but other methods such as the use of sandpaper, bottle tops, buckles, finger nails and artificial substances are proscribed. Picking the seam has long been common (and illegal) practice, but the relative novelty of reverse swing has brought with it new methods of cheating. Imran Khan, Waqar Younis and Wasim Akram developed and perfected the art of reverse swing by roughening one side of the ball and bowling a full length, and doing it in a legal way. If roughing one side is achieved by keeping the ball dry and bowling cross-seam on to the same side, or throwing a non-rotating ball on to one side, then that is fair enough, but it takes time and if the ball rotates, there is a danger of roughing both sides, which is no use to any bowler. So it is tempting to resort to other methods which are quicker and more effective.

Matters came to a head with Pakistan in The Oval Test of 2006 when umpire Darrell Hair, convinced that Pakistan were interfering with the condition of the ball, awarded five penalty runs to England and, under ICC regulations, gave the batsmen the choice of a replacement ball. Affronted, Pakistan declined to take the field after tea. The England batsmen, Ian Bell and Paul Collingwood, followed the umpires to the crease and when Pakistan remained in their dressing room, umpires Hair and Billy Doctrove removed the bails and awarded the match to England under Law 21.3. Negotiations continued well into the evening, but the result stood.

The image of the game was seriously damaged. It was a high-profile match and with a little less intransigence, the matter could have been resolved more amicably. Firstly, Darrell Hair and his colleague were absolutely correct in their interpretation of the law, but they might have handled the matter more diplomatically. I have always felt that the best umpires are those who interact with the players rather than just impose the laws in the style of a football referee. Secondly, the Pakistan captain Inzamam-ul-Haq and the management team might have been more flexible. If they felt the umpires were wrong, then surely the correct course of action was to play out the match and put their case to the ICC afterwards. Finally, the paying public were kept completely in the dark. Any grievances could have been aired in the captain's match report. As it was, the saga dragged on. The ICC first changed the result to a draw, then changed it back again to an England win. It was a sad period for cricket.

The Tour Manager was Zaheer Abbas, now President of the ICC. Shaharyar Khan, now Chairman of the Pakistan Cricket Board, was also part of the drama. Their part in the decision not to continue the match was not right and certainly did no good to Pakistan cricket. Since then, however, both are desperately keen to improve Pakistan's reputation internationally. They are hampered by the politicians and extremists, but in terms of cricket, they have the support of more than a billion people on the subcontinent with a passion for the game.

At the present time, it looks as though regular international cricket in Pakistan is unlikely to be possible for a few years. Since partition – and indeed before – Pakistan has been politically volatile. For most of the twentieth century, conflict was mainly internal. That was all to change after 9/11 when President Bush looked at the map and discovered that Pakistan was adjacent to Afghanistan and a potential ally in his 'war on terror'. Thereafter, neither India nor Pakistan – and increasingly anywhere else – are exempt from attack, as Islamic terrorism continues to increase. The repercussions of the attack on the Sri Lanka team bus in March 2009 will be felt for some time.

Against this background cricket continued, but Pakistan's international game was obliged to move to the UAE. The team needed a strong leader and found one eventually in Misbah-ul-Haq. Having played regularly in the early years of the twenty-first century, he took over after the disgrace of Salman Butt and stabilised the national team in a similar way to Graeme Smith after the demise of Hansie Cronje.

Meanwhile world cricket remains the poorer in the absence of cricket between two great rivals. Pakistan and India are young countries without the cricket history of either England or Australia, but the passion for the game on the subcontinent means that regular series between Pakistan and India would rival or even exceed the Ashes in popular appeal. Despite political opposition in Mumbai, Zaheer Abbas, in his capacity of President of ICC, is helping in the effort to restore relations

Geoffrey Boycott recently said that the pattern of selection in Pakistan is to ban players for life, then bring them back after five years. It was said in jest, but over the years, events have demonstrated that there is more than a grain of truth in it. After all, it happened to me!

In his autobiography, Imran Khan says, 'The history of Pakistan cricket is one of nepotism, inefficiency, corruption and constant bickering. It is also the story of players who have risen above the mire. A cricketer needs immense talent, belief in himself and sheer luck to survive the political maze of our cricket.'

That was in 1988. Almost thirty years down the road, little has changed. Let us hope that there will be those who continue to rise above the mire.

Family first – with my son, Sam.

Acknowledgements

I am grateful to all those I played with and against who have provided me with the memories and experiences which form the basis of these chapters. Thanks also to the two great ladies in my life, Gloria and Puchi, for their love and wonderful support over the years.

In terms of producing this book, thanks to Keith Booth for his help in writing the book and filling in the background facts and statistics, and to Scott Reeves at Chequered Flag Publishing for his meticulous editing and for rearranging his schedule to ensure the book hit the market in time for the Pakistan tour of England in 2016.

YOUNIS AHMED ...
prolific run-maker.

Another addition to my total of first-class runs.

Statistics

TEST MATCHES

BATTING

	Matches	Inns	NO	High	Runs	Ave
1961/62 v NZ (home)						
	2	4	0	62	89	22.25
1986/87 v India (away)						
	2	3	1	40	88	44.00
TOTAL	**4**	**7**	**1**	**62**	**177**	**29.50**

BOWLING

	Overs	Maidens	Runs	Wickets	Average
1986/87 v India (away)					
	1	0	6	0	-

FIRST CLASS MATCHES

BATTING

		Matches	Innings	Not Outs	Highest	Runs	Ave
1961/62	Pakistan	1	2	0	14	14	7.00
1963/64	Pakistan	1	1	0	28	28	28.00
1964/65	Pakistan	8	12	1	122	296	26.90
1965	Surrey	1	2	0	66	87	43.50
1967	Surrey	19	29	4	103	639	25.56
1967/68	Pakistan	3	5	0	58	152	30.40
1968	Surrey	22	35	8	96	749	27.74
1969	Surrey	28	46	9	127	1760	47.56
1969/70	Pakistan	10	17	2	147*	466	31.06
1969	Jamaica	1	2	0	14	14	7.00
1970	Surrey	25	46	7	120*	1588	40.71
1970/71	Pakistan	3	5	0	47	107	21.40
1971	Surrey	27	47	6	138*	1485	36.21
1972	Surrey	21	38	3	143	1232	35.20
1972/73	S Aus	6	11	0	69	289	26.27
1973	Surrey	24	38	7	155*	1620	52.25
1973/74	S Africa	6	10	3	123	351	50.14
1974	Surrey	19	33	4	116	907	31.27
1974/75	S Africa	4	8	1	154	388	55.42
1975	Surrey	21	38	3	183*	1314	37.54
1975/76	S Africa	1	2	0	25	42	21.00
1976	Surrey	21	41	5	161	1439	39.97
1977	Surrey	20	34	3	61*	786	25.35
1978	Surrey	15	23	4	72	514	27.05
1979	Worcs	22	30	8	221*	1539	69.95
1980	Worcs	21	33	6	121*	1018	37.70
1981	Worcs	22	39	8	116	1637	52.80
1982	Worcs	18	29	6	122	1427	54.21
1983	Worcs	2	2	2	35*	45	-
1984	Glam	21	35	4	158*	1369	44.16
1985	Glam	22	30	8	177	1421	64.59
1986	Glam	15	23	2	105*	845	40.23
1986/87	Pak/Ind	10	16	4	110	685	57.08
TOTAL		**460**	**762**	**118**	**221***	**26,073**	**40.48**

FIRST CLASS MATCHES

BOWLING

		Overs	Maidens	Runs	Wickets	Ave
1963/64	Pakistan	6	1	26	0	-
1964/65	Pakistan	38	3	129	2	64.50
1967	Surrey	86	30	170	1	170.00
1967/68	Pakistan	5	3	137	3	45.66
1968	Surrey	23	4	80	1	80.00
1969	Surrey	38	10	100	5	20.00
1969/70	Pakistan	6.5	0	35	3	11.66
1970	Surrey	5.5	2	15	1	15.00
1971	Surrey	7	4	20	2	10.00
1972	Surrey	2	2	0	0	-
1972/73	S Aus	34 (8-ball)	5	122	2	61.00
1973	Surrey	5	1	17	0	-
1973/74	S Africa	8	1	33	0	-
1974	Surrey	6	2	11	0	-
1975	Surrey	15	8	20	4	5.00
1976	Surrey	15.1	1	62	0	-
1977	Surrey	30	13	80	3	26.66
1978	Surrey	9	2	27	0	-
1979	Worcs	92.5	22	229	8	28.62
1980	Worcs	19	1	95	1	95.00
1981	Worcs	62	9	183	3	61.00
1982	Worcs	5	1	14	0	-
1984	Glam	12	3	34	0	-
1985	Glam	74.4	22	178	2	89.00
1986	Glam	20	4	82	0	-
1986/87	Pak/Ind	66	11	202	8	25.25
TOTAL		**676.2** **+34.8 8-ball**	**165**	**2101**	**49**	**42.87**

FIRST-CLASS CENTURIES
46 in 460 matches

221*	Worcestershire v Nottinghamshire (Trent Bridge) 1979
183*	Surrey v Worcestershire (Worcester) 1975
177	Glamorgan v Middlesex (Cardiff) 1985
170	Worcestershire v Kent (Canterbury) 1979
161	Surrey v Nottinghamshire (Oval) 1976
158*	Glamorgan v Oxford University (The Parks) 1984
155*	Surrey v Warwickshire (Oval) 1973
154	International Wanderers v Transvaal (Wanderers) 1974/75
152*	Worcestershire v Warwickshire (Worcester) 1979
147*	PIA A v Rawalpindi (Rawalpindi) 1969/70
143*	Glamorgan v Hampshire (Cardiff) 1985
143	Surrey v Middlesex (Oval) 1972
141*	Surrey v New Zealanders (Oval) 1973
138*	Surrey v Leicestershire (Leicester) 1971
127*	Surrey v Derbyshire (Oval) 1967
123	DH Robins XI v Transvaal (Wanderers) 1973/74
122*	Surrey v Gloucestershire (Bristol) 1969
122	Lahore Education Board v Rawalpindi 1964/65
122	Worcestershire v Leicestershire (Worcester) 1982
122	Glamorgan v Sussex (Hove) 1984
121*	Worcestershire v Warwickshire (Birmingham) 1980
120*	Surrey v Somerset (Oval) 1970
118*	Glamorgan v Australians (Neath) 1985
117	Surrey v Derbyshire (Chesterfield) 1973
116	Surrey v Leicestershire (Oval) 1974
116	Surrey v Sussex (Hove) 1975
116	Worcestershire v Surrey (Oval) 1981
114	Worcestershire v Nottinghamshire (Worcester) 1982
113*	Surrey v Gloucestershire (Oval) 1969
113	Glamorgan v Oxford University (The Parks) 1985
112*	Worcestershire v Gloucestershire (Worcester) 1982
112	Surrey v Northamptonshire (Oval) 1970
112	Surrey v Worcestershire (Oval) 1972
110	Worcestershire v Warwickshire (Edgbaston) 1982
110	Lahore City v United Bank (Lahore) 1986/87

109*   Surrey v Oxford University (The Parks) 1969
109   Worcestershire v Nottinghamshire (Cleethorpes) 1980
107   Worcestershire v Surrey (Guildford) 1979
107   Worcestershire v Derbyshire (Chesterfield) 1981
106*   Worcestershire v Warwickshire (Edgbaston)1981
106   Surrey v Yorkshire (Oval) 1973
105*   Glamorgan v Sussex (Cardiff) 1986
103*   Pakistanis v Delhi (Delhi) 1986/87
103   Surrey v Derbyshire (Oval) 1967
101*   Surrey v Warwickshire (Edgbaston) 1969
100*   Glamorgan v Worcestershire (Worcester) 1985

LIMITED OVERS CENTURIES
7 in 326 matches

115   Worcestershire v Yorkshire (Worcester) 1980
113   Surrey v Warwickshire (Edgbaston) 1976
113   Worcestershire v Middlesex (Lord's) 1979
107   Worcestershire v Surrey (Worcester) 1979
103*   Glamorgan v Derbyshire (Ebbw Vale) 1984
101*   Surrey v Kent (Canterbury) 1974
100   Worcestershire v Leicestershire (Leicester) 1979

Index

Also from Chequered Flag Publishing:

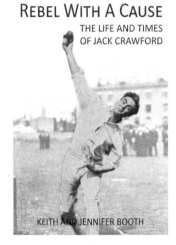

REBEL WITH A CAUSE

THE LIFE AND TIMES OF JACK CRAWFORD

by Keith and Jennifer Booth

Prodigy. Record breaker. Enigma.

Jack Crawford, described as the greatest ever schoolboy cricketer, blazed into the Surrey team at the age of seventeen and broke a host of records: the youngest Surrey centurion and double centurion, the youngest player to achieve the double of 100 wickets and 1,000 runs in a season. He became the youngest cricketer to play for England and a Wisden Cricketer of the Year.

Yet, not long after his twenty-first birthday, he played the last of his twelve Test matches. He fell out with the Surrey committee, then with the South Australian Cricket Association and Otago Cricket Association after moving to play in the Southern Hemisphere. What went wrong?

Crawford's career raises many questions which have only been partially answered. Why did he stand up to the Surrey committee? What happened in Australia and New Zealand? Did he try to dodge the Great War? Was he a bigamist? Now, thanks to Keith and Jennifer Booth's meticulous research, the truth is fully known.

Also from Chequered Flag Publishing:

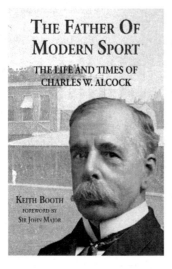

THE FATHER OF MODERN SPORT

THE LIFE AND TIMES OF CHARLES W. ALCOCK

by Keith Booth
Foreword by Sir John Major

SHORTLISTED FOR CRICKET SOCIETY BOOK OF THE YEAR 2002

A model Victorian sporting all-rounder, Charles Alcock was a prime mover in the development of both football and cricket as the world's biggest sports.

As a player, he was the first ever footballer to be ruled offside, the captain of the first FA Cup winners and played club cricket to a high standard.

As Secretary of the FA, Alcock was one of the men responsible for the first ever football international and was the driving force behind the creation of the FA Cup in 1871. In cricket, he arranged the first Test match in Britain, between England and Australia at The Oval in 1880.

Close attention to detail combined with a breadth of vision to change the sporting world – this is the definitive biography of the nineteenth century's most important sports administrator.

Also from Chequered Flag Publishing:

THE CHAMPION BAND

The First English Cricket Tour

by Scott Reeves

CRICKET WEB BEST NEW WRITER 2014

In 1859, twelve cricketers left Liverpool to embark on the first overseas tour by a representative England side. Their destination was the place where cricket looked most likely to flourish: Canada and the United States.

It was not an easy trip – the English players experienced death on the high seas, were threatened at gunpoint and sensed unrest in the pre-Civil War USA.

Led by George Parr, the English tourists came up against the best of the New World cricketers. Some of the locals would go on to pioneer the sport that ultimately caused the death of North American cricket: baseball.

A gripping account featuring original research, THE CHAMPION BAND tells the fascinating story of the first English cricket tour.

INNOVATIVE AND EXCITING SPORTS BOOKS

Chequered Flag
PUBLISHING

www.chequeredflagpublishing.co.uk